Let's Read Aloud & Learn English for Science

音読で学ぶ基礎英語≪サイエンス編≫

Teruhiko Kadoyama
Simon Capper

SEIBIDO

photographs by
iStockphoto
ゲッティイメージズ
Alamy Stock Photo

Let's Read Aloud & Learn English for Science

は し が き

　本書は、「音読」や「筆写」といった、一見地味ですが確実に英語力アップにつながる練習法を取り入れた総合英語テキストで、『音読で始める基礎英語』シリーズの第5弾に当たるものです。前4作同様、基礎的な語彙や文法の確認に重点を置いていますが、本作は理工系学部の大学生を主人公としたストーリー仕立てになっていますので、実験やレポート、期末試験など、キャンパスライフに密着した表現を数多く学ぶことができるはずです。

　「英語をペラペラ話せるようになりたい」と願う人は多いですが、授業や自宅での学習で実際にどれだけ英語を音読する練習をしてきたでしょうか？　何度も音読しなければやはり英語が口からすぐに出てくるようにはなりませんし、実際に英文を書いてみるという作業は表現を確認し定着させる上で非常に効果的です。デジタル全盛な時代にあえてこうしたアナログ的な練習方法を提唱するのは、やはり1番効果が実感しやすい方法だと思うからです。

　しかし、本書はアナログ的な面だけを重視したテキストでは決してありません。本書はWeb英語学習システムのTESTUDY（テスタディ）※に対応していますので、パソコンやスマートフォンを使ったモバイル・ラーニングが可能です。アナログとデジタルのそれぞれ良い点を皆さんの英語学習に活かしてほしいと願っています。　※教員の指示に従って学習・受験してください。

　本書の刊行にあたっては、成美堂の佐野英一郎氏、そして編集部の工藤隆志氏、萩原美奈子氏に多大なご尽力を賜りました。衷心よりお礼申し上げます。

角山照彦
Simon Capper

本書の構成と使い方

本書は 15 ユニットからなり、各ユニットの構成は次のようになっています。

 ## Warm-up

授業前に確認しておこう！

授業で聞く対話の中に出てくる重要単語や表現、そして文法項目を取り上げていますので、授業の予習としてやっておきましょう。

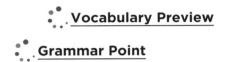

 ## Let's Listen!

会話の大意を聞き取ろう！

キャンパスライフを舞台にした対話を聞いてみましょう。対話の大意が理解できているかを試す問題が用意されています。

 ## Let's Check & Read Aloud!

音読してみよう！

空欄補充問題を設けていますので、Let's Listen! で聞いた対話をもう1度聞いて空欄を埋めてみましょう。内容を確認したら、音読、そしてパートナーとロールプレイ（役割練習）をしてみましょう。QR コードからアクセスできるオンライン動画を用意していますので、ぜひ自宅学習でも積極的に取り入れてください。そうすればその効果が実感できることでしょう。

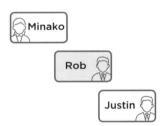

 ## Grammar

文法に強くなろう！

Warm-up で取り上げた文法項目の確認問題です。文法に苦手意識のある方はこのページでしっかり復習をしておきましょう。

Let's Read!

読解力を高めよう！

天体、人体、元素など、科学トピックを扱ったパッセージを読んでみましょう。大意が理解できているかを試す問題が用意されています。

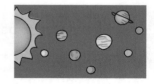

Challenge Yourself!

リスニング力を試そう！

英語の資格試験としてよく知られている TOEIC L&R® と似た形式のリスニング問題を用意しました。試験を意識した実践的な演習をしてみましょう。

(A)　　　(B)　　　(C)

Let's Read Aloud & Write!

音読筆写で覚えよう！

最後に授業のまとめとして、学習した対話を音読筆写してみましょう。日本語訳だけを見ながら英文がスラスラと書けるようになることが目標です。

Let's Review！

しっかり復習しよう！

巻末に文法と表現の復習コーナーを用意しています。日本語の文を見てすぐさま対応する英文を言ってみるという Quick Response（即時反応）のトレーニングで、学習した内容がしっかり身についているかどうか確かめましょう。

TESTUDY

本書は TESTUDY（＝ TEST ＋ STUDY）という「e-learning ＋ オンラインテスト」システムに対応しています。各 Unit の復習やオンラインテストの受験が可能です。教員の指示に従って学習・受験してください。

Table of Contents

UNIT	タイトル	会話テーマ	文法	言語機能	読解テーマ
01 p.8	Everything is new to me.	スモールトーク	be動詞・疑問詞	話しかける 自己紹介する	天体
02 p.14	Are you in any clubs?	クラブ活動	一般動詞（現在形）	人を誘う 別れ際の挨拶	数と計算
03 p.20	Let me introduce a new member to you.	専攻	一般動詞（過去形）	人を紹介する 確信を示す	単位1（長さ）
04 p.26	I'm looking for a part-time job.	アルバイト	進行形	詳細を尋ねる 依頼する	単位2（音の強さ）
05 p.32	What are you going to do?	学校行事	未来表現	予定を尋ねる 驚きを示す	建築
06 p.38	Could you take a look at this slide?	プレゼン準備1	助動詞	状況を説明する 助言する	グラフ1（円グラフ）
07 p.44	I'm so frustrated.	プレゼン準備2	受動態	感謝する お礼への返答	グラフ2（棒グラフ）
08 p.50	It's something we need to think about.	情報倫理	現在完了形	経験を尋ねる 可能性を示す	人体1（骨）
09 p.56	I'm ready to start the experiment.	実験	不定詞	注意する 確認する	単位3（温度）
10 p.62	I totally forgot to write my report.	レポート	形容詞・副詞	近況を尋ねる 理解を示す	人体2（血液）
11 p.68	This is still a beta version.	アプリ開発	分詞	興味を示す 例示する	ロボット
12 p.74	I'm thinking of joining the course.	語学研修	動名詞	意見を尋ねる 励ます	元素1（元素周期表）

主な登場人物

Minako
大学 1 年生

Rob
姉妹校からの
交換留学生

Justin
姉妹校からの
交換留学生

Unit 01 Everything is new to me.

文法 ▶be 動詞

ミナコは、学生食堂で交換留学生のロブに話しかけます。会話では、話しかけたり、自己紹介したりする際の表現を学びます。また、文法では be 動詞（現在形・過去形）と疑問詞、読解では天体にそれぞれ焦点を当てて学習します。

 Warm-up　　　　　　　　　　　　授業前に確認しておこう！

Vocabulary Preview
🎵 1-02

1〜10 の語句の意味として適切なものを a 〜 j の中から選びましょう。

1. freshman	_____	a. 2 年生
2. exchange	_____	b. 本当に、確かに
3. engineering	_____	c. 工学
4. must	_____	d. 共通に、共同で
5. seem	_____	e. 1 年生
6. in common	_____	f. 偶然の一致
7. indeed	_____	g. （大学の）専攻、（〜の）専攻学生
8. sophomore	_____	h. 〜のように見える
9. coincidence	_____	i. 〜に違いない
10. major	_____	j. 交換

ビートに乗って 1〜10 の語句を発音してみましょう。

Grammar Point : be 動詞

I'm a freshman, and my major is engineering.　　（私は大学 1 年生で、専攻は工学です）

My father was also an engineering major when he was in college.

（父も大学時代は工学を専攻していました）

　be 動詞は名詞や形容詞、場所を表す語句が後に続いて「〜である、〜にいる」という意味を表し、主語によっていろいろと形が変わります。また、「〜だった、〜にいた」と過去を表す場合も同じく変化します。下の表の空欄に枠の中から適切な動詞の形を選んで表を完成させましょう。

話し手のことを 1 人称、相手方を 2 人称、それ以外の人たちを 3 人称と言います。

	主　　　　　語		現在形	過去形
1 人称	単数（私）	I	*am*	
	複数（私たち）	we		
2 人称	単数（あなた）	you		
	複数（あなたたち）			
3 人称	単数（彼、彼女、それ）	he, she, it		
	複数（彼ら、それら）	they		

am ✓
is
are
was
were

「〜ではない」という否定文にするときは、be 動詞のすぐ後に not をつけます。また、「〜ですか？」という疑問文にするには be 動詞を主語の前に持ってきます。下の例文の日本語訳を完成させながら確認しましょう。

> is not = isn't, are not = aren't のように会話では短縮形がよく使われます。ただし、I am not は通常 I'm not となります。× I amn't

Earth **isn't** the only planet in the solar system.　（　　　　　　　　　　　）

Is Mercury the closest planet to the sun?　（　　　　　　　　　　　）

なお、疑問文を作る際には、when や where などの**疑問詞**がよく使われますが、これらは通常疑問文の始めに置かれます。下の表で確認した後、例文の日本語訳を完成させましょう。

what	何	who	誰	how	どのように
where	どこへ（で）	why	なぜ	how far	どれくらいの距離
when	いつ	which	どれ	how long	どれくらいの時間

"**What**'s your major?" "Engineering. How about yours?"
（　　　　　　　　　　　）

"**How long** is a class period at this university?" "It's 90 minutes."
（　　　　　　　　　　　）

be 動詞は、単に「（〜は）…である」と言う場合だけでなく、≪ be going to ... ≫の形で未来表現、≪ be ＋ -ing ≫の形で進行形、≪ be ＋過去分詞≫の形で受動態など、様々な表現で使われます。基本をしっかりと確認しておきましょう。

 Let's Listen!　　　　　　　会話の大意を聞き取ろう！

ミナコとロブの会話を聞いて、質問に対する答えとして最も適切なものを（A）〜（C）の中から1つ選びましょう。 1-03

Question 1　Is Rob a first-year student?

(A) Yes, he is.
(B) No, he's a second-year student.
(C) No, he's a third-year student.

Question 2　Is this the first time for him to visit Japan?

(A) Yes, it is.
(B) No, this is his second visit.
(C) No, this is his third visit.

Question 3　What is true of Minako?

(A) Her major is different from Rob's.
(B) She's a second-year student.
(C) She lives alone near the campus.

1. スクリプトを見ながら会話をもう１度聞き、下線部に当てはまる表現を書き入れましょう。（下線部には単語が２つ入ります） 1-03
2. 内容を確認して、全文を音読してみましょう。
3. ミナコとロブの役割をパートナーと一緒に演じてみましょう。

Let's Practice the Roleplay!

Minako's Role　　Rob's Role

最後にQRコードから動画にアクセスして
各自ロールプレイの練習をしましょう。

Minako speaks to Rob in the cafeteria.

| Minako | Hi, I'm Minako. You ① ＿＿＿＿＿＿＿＿＿ an exchange student from our sister university. Nice to meet you. |

| Rob | Yes, I'm Rob. Nice to meet you, too. |

| Minako | ② ＿＿＿＿＿＿＿＿＿ freshman, right? |

| Rob | No, I'm a sophomore. How ③ ＿＿＿＿＿＿＿＿＿ ? |

| Minako | I'm a freshman, and my ④ ＿＿＿＿＿＿＿＿＿ earth science. |

| Rob | Oh, ⑤ ＿＿＿＿＿＿＿＿＿ earth science, too. What a coincidence! |

| Minako | Yes, indeed. Is this your ⑥ ＿＿＿＿＿＿＿＿＿ to Japan? |

| Rob | Yes, it is. Everything's new to me. |

| Minako | I started ⑦ ＿＿＿＿＿＿＿＿＿ near the campus a week ago, so everything is new to me, too. |

| Rob | Well, we seem to have a lot ⑧ ＿＿＿＿＿＿＿＿＿ . |

| Minako | Yes, we do! |

💡 **聞き取りのヒント**

"Nice to meet you." の meet you が「ミーチュ」のように発音されることはよく知られていますが、この meet のように [t] で終わる単語のすぐ後に you のような [j] で始まる単語が来ると、２つの音が一緒になって [tʃ]（チュ）という別の音に変わってしまいます。また、did のように、[d] で終わる単語のすぐ後に [j] で始まる単語が来た場合も、２つの音が一緒になって [dʒ]（ヂュ）という別の音に変わります。こうした現象を音の同化と呼びます。

 # Grammar

 文法に強くなろう！

A. 例にならい、カッコ内に適切な be 動詞を書き入れましょう。

例　What (_are_) diamonds made of?

1. All things on Earth (　　　　) made of matter.

2. All matter (　　　　) made of chemical elements.

3. My parents studied at the same college and they (　　　　) both science majors.

4. I studied in Australia for a month when I (　　　　) a high school student.

B. 例にならい、A と B の対話が成り立つように枠の中から適切な疑問詞を選んで文を完成させましょう。

例　A: _How long_ is a class period at this university?
　　B: It's 90 minutes.

what
when
who
where
why
how
how long ✓
how much
how many

1. A: ＿＿＿＿＿＿ was Earth formed?

B: About 4.5 billion years ago.

2. A: ＿＿＿＿＿＿ old is Earth?

B: It's about 4.5 billion years old.

3. A: ＿＿＿＿＿＿ is the size of Earth in diameter?

B: It's 12,742 kilometers.

4. A: ＿＿＿＿＿＿ planets are there in the solar system?

B: There are eight.

C. 日本語の意味に合うようにカッコ内の語句を並べ替え、英文を完成させましょう。ただし、文の始めにくる単語も小文字にしてあり、1 つ余分な語句が含まれています。

1. 月はどれくらい離れていますか？

(are / is / the / far away / how / Moon)？

_____

2. 月は地球から平均距離 384,400 キロ離れています。

(are / is / an average / of / the Moon / 384,400 kilometers) away from the Earth.

_____

3. 惑星はなぜすべて丸いのですか？

(all of / are / is / the planets / why / round)？

_____

4. 地球の表面の約 71％ は海です。

(is / 71 percent / surface / Earth's / about / of / was) sea.

_____

Let's Read!

次のパッセージを読み、その内容について 1〜3 の質問に答えましょう。

 1-04

What Is Earth?

What do you know about your home planet—Earth? Scientists believe that Earth was formed about 4.5 billion years ago. It is the third-closest planet to the sun in our solar system. Only Mercury and Venus are closer. Earth is also the fifth-largest planet in the system.

Earth is an ocean planet, and water covers about 71% of its surface. It is the only planet known to have life on it. On Earth, everything is just right for life to exist. It's warm, but not too warm. Cold, but not so cold that the water freezes. For this reason, it's said to be in the sun's "Goldilocks Zone."

---

1. According to scientists, Earth was formed about _____ years ago.

   (A) 4,500,000

   (B) 45,000,000

   (C) 4,500,000,000

2. _____ planets are bigger than Earth.

   (A) Two

   (B) Three

   (C) Four

3. _____ of Earth's surface is covered with water.

   (A) About a half

   (B) More than two thirds

   (C) About four fifths

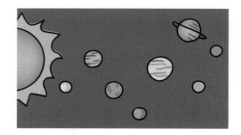

 Notes

exist: 存在する   Goldilocks Zone: ゴルディロックスゾーン（居住可能地帯）

according to: 〜によれば

Challenge Yourself!

Part I　Photographs

(A)〜(C) の英文を聞き、写真の描写として最も適切なものを選びましょう。　 1-05

1.

　　　(A)　　(B)　　(C)

2.

　　　(A)　　(B)　　(C)

Part II　Question-Response

最初に聞こえてくる英文に対する応答として最も適切なものを（A）〜（C）の中から選びましょう。　 1-06

3.　(A)　　(B)　　(C)

4.　(A)　　(B)　　(C)

Part III　Short Conversations

会話を聞き、下の英文が会話の内容と合っていれば T（True）、間違っていれば F（False）を○で囲みましょう。　 1-07

5. Both the man and woman are second-year students.　　　　T　　　F

6. The woman wants to be a biology teacher.　　　　T　　　F

 Let's Read Aloud & Write!

授業のまとめとして、今日学習した対話文を３回書き写してしっかり覚えましょう。１度英文を声に出して読んでから書き写すと頭に残りやすくなります。

┤ 今日のまとめ ├

英語で答えられますか？　　What is your major?

Unit 02 Are you in any clubs?

文法 一般動詞（現在形）

学生食堂でミナコとロブの話が続きます。会話では、人を誘ったり、別れ際に挨拶したりする際の表現を学びます。また、文法では**一般動詞（現在形）**、読解では**数と計算**に焦点を当てて学習します。

Warm-up

授業前に確認しておこう！

Vocabulary Preview

🎵 1-08

1～10 の語句の意味として適切なものを a～j の中から選びましょう。

1. sound	＿＿＿	a.	国際的な
2. continue	＿＿＿	b.	2 回、2 度
3. kid	＿＿＿	c.	計算する
4. belong to	＿＿＿	d.	休憩室
5. calculate	＿＿＿	e.	～に所属する
6. international	＿＿＿	f.	～しなければならない
7. introduce	＿＿＿	g.	からかう
8. have to	＿＿＿	h.	紹介する
9. lounge	＿＿＿	i.	～に聞こえる、～に思える
10. twice	＿＿＿	j.	続ける

ビートに乗って 1～10 の語句を発音してみましょう。

Grammar Point : 一般動詞（現在形）

I <u>belong</u> to the mathematics club. （私は数学クラブに所属しています）
My father <u>teaches</u> science at a college. （父は大学で科学を教えています）

be 動詞以外の動詞を**一般動詞**と呼び、現在の状況や習慣を示す場合、**現在形**を用います。ほとんどの場合、現在形は動詞のもとの形（＝**原形**）と同じですが、主語が 3 人称で単数の場合には語尾に -s や -es がつきます。下の表の空欄に適切な動詞の形を書き入れて確認しましょう。

> a, i, u, e, o のことを**母音字**、それ以外を**子音字**と言います。

1. 多くの動詞	語尾に -s をつける	like → likes	want → wants
2. -s, -sh, -ch, -x, <子音字 +o> で終わる動詞	語尾に -es をつける	go → goes	pass →
3. <子音字 +y> で終わる動詞	y を i に変えて -es をつける	fly → flies	carry →
4. 例外的な動詞	不規則な変化をする	have→ has	

一般動詞を使った現在形の文を疑問文にするときは、文の始めに do を持ってきます。また否定文にするには動詞のすぐ前に don't（=do not）をつけます。主語が 3 人称で単数の場合は does や doesn't を使い、動詞は語尾の -s や -es を外して原形に戻します。下の例文の日本語訳を完成させながら確認しましょう。

Do you walk to school, or take a school bus?

(　　　　　　　　　　　　　　　　　　　　　　　　　　　)

My sister **doesn't** belong to any club, but I want to join the science club.

(　　　　　　　　　　　　　　　　　　　　　　　　　　　)

> 「今〜している」のように、現在の動作を表す場合は、**現在進行形**（Unit 4）を用います。

　また、現在形というと現時点だけを示すと考えがちですが、実際には下記の表のように、**現在を中心とした幅広い時間**を示します。**普段のことを話す場合に使う形**と覚えておくとよいでしょう。下の例文の日本語訳を完成させながら確認しましょう。

現在の状態	I love driving. I feel great. (　　　　　　　　　)	現在
習慣的な動作	Our club meets twice a week. (　　　　　　　　　)	現在
一般的な事実・真理	The sun rises in the east. (　　　　　　　　　)	現在

 Let's Listen!　　　　　　　　会話の大意を聞き取ろう！

ミナコとロブの会話を聞いて、質問に対する答えとして最も適切なものを（A）〜（C）の中から 1 つ選びましょう。　　 1-09

Question ①　Does Minako belong to any club now?

(A) Yes, she belongs to the mathematics club.
(B) Yes, she belongs to the international exchange club.
(C) No, she doesn't.

Question ②　How often does the club meet?

(A) Once a week
(B) Twice a week
(C) Three times a week

Question ③　What does Rob tell Minako?

(A) That he can introduce her to the members
(B) That he wants to join the club
(C) Where the student lounge is

Let's Check & Read Aloud!

音読してみよう！

1. スクリプトを見ながら会話をもう１度聞き、下線部に当てはまる表現を書き入れましょう。（下線部には単語が２つ入ります）　 1-09
2. 内容を確認して、全文を音読してみましょう。
3. ミナコとロブの役割をパートナーと一緒に演じてみましょう。

Let's Practice the Roleplay!

Rob's Role　　Minako's Role

Minako and Rob continue to talk at the school cafeteria.

Rob: How do you like your new school?

Minako: ① _____ . I have some new friends now.

Rob: Oh, that's good. Are you in any clubs?

Minako: No, not yet. But I'm ② _____ the mathematics club.

Rob: No kidding! I'm a member of the math club. ③ _____ you join us? You can have a great time there.

Minako: Sounds great. How ④ _____ the club meet?

Rob: Twice a week, Tuesday and Friday at 6 p.m.

Minako: That's fine with me. ⑤ _____ come this Friday?

Rob: Of course. Come to the student lounge at 6:00. I can ⑥ _____ to the members.

Minako: Oh, thank you very much. I'll be there.

Rob: Well, I ⑦ _____ go now. It was nice talking to you.

Minako: Nice talking to you, too. See ⑧ _____ .

💡 **音読のヒント**

"Thank you." [θǽŋkjù] は非常によく使う表現ですから、カタカナ英語で「サンキュー」とならないように、しっかり練習しましょう。th の発音記号 [θ] は前歯で舌の先を軽く噛んだ状態で「スー」っと息を吐く音で、カタカナではうまく書き表すことができません。舌を軽く出して素早く引きながら発音します。「サァンキュゥ」のような感じです。

Grammar

A. 例にならい、枠の中から適切な単語を選び、必要な場合は適切な形にして次の1〜4の文を完成させましょう。

例 One plus two (*is*) three.

1. Five minus two (　　　　　) three.

2. When we (　　　　　) seven and four, we get eleven.

3. When we (　　　　　) five from nine, we get four.

4. When you (　　　　　) three by five, you get fifteen.

> multiply
> be ✓
> add
> subtract
> equal

B. 例にならい、カッコ内の動詞を肯定・否定・疑問のいずれか適切な形に変えて文を完成させましょう。4は主語として you を補いましょう。

例 My sister likes math, but I <u>don't like</u> it. (like)

1. I enjoy our science project, but my partner _____ to enjoy it. (seem)

2. The difference between 9 and 5 _____ 4. (be)

3. Roy is good with numbers. He never _____ a mistake in his calculations. (make)

4. "What _____ if you add four and seven?" "We get eleven." (get)

C. 計算式の内容に合うようにカッコ内の語句を並べ替え、英文を完成させましょう。ただし、文の始めにくる単語も小文字にしてあり、1つ余分な語句が含まれています。

1. 5 × 4 = 20　Five (is / four / twenty / time / times).

_____

2. 4 × 2 = 8　Four (by / eight / two / plus / equals / multiplied).

_____

3. 20 ÷ 4 = 5　Twenty (divided / with / five / four / equals / by).

_____

4. 9 − 6 = 3　Six (by / subtracted / is / nine / three / from).

_____

Tips

四則演算の読み方

四則演算		記号	記号の読み方	計算結果	
足し算	addition	+	plus	和	sum
引き算	subtraction	−	minus	差	difference
掛け算	multiplication	×	times, multiplied by	積	product
割り算	division	÷	divided by	商	quotient

17

 # Let's Read!

 読解力を高めよう！

次のパッセージを読み、その内容について 1～3 の質問に答えましょう。 1-10

Real World Math

When am I going to use math? Students often wonder if, when, and how they will ever use math in "real life" situations. However, the truth is that we use math all the time! For example, at your local supermarket you find people using math in everyday life. Each time you calculate the price per unit and <u>estimate</u> the final price, you're using math in your shopping experience. Math also helps you build things. Ask any architect or construction worker. They'll tell you how important math is when it comes to building anything. Remember, math is everywhere. It's all around us.

---

1. According to the passage, students often wonder _____ .

   (A) if they can find people using math in everyday life

   (B) if they can build things without math

   (C) if they have a chance to use math outside of class

2. The underlined word "estimate" means _____ .

   (A) guess

   (B) ask

   (C) lower

3. What is the main topic of this passage?

   (A) The importance of grocery stores

   (B) How to solve math problems

   (C) Use of math in our daily life

 Notes

per: ～につき   architect: 建築家   when it comes to: ～のことになると
underlined: 下線が引かれた

Challenge Yourself!

Part I Photographs

(A) ～ (C) の英文を聞き、写真の描写として最も適切なものを選びましょう。 1-11

1.

(A)　　　(B)　　　(C)

2.

(A)　　　(B)　　　(C)

Part II Question-Response

最初に聞こえてくる英文に対する応答として最も適切なものを (A) ～ (C) の中から選びましょう。 1-12

3.　(A)　　　(B)　　　(C)

4.　(A)　　　(B)　　　(C)

Part III Short Conversations

会話を聞き、下の英文が会話の内容と合っていれば T (True)、間違っていれば F (False) を○で囲みましょう。 1-13

5. The woman is a new member of the club.　　　　T　　　F

6. The woman asks the man when he joined the club.　　T　　　F

 ## Let's Read Aloud & Write!

授業のまとめとして、今日学習した対話文を 3 回書き写してしっかり覚えましょう。1 度英文を声に出して読んでから書き写すと頭に残りやすくなります。

┤ 今日のまとめ ├

英語で答えられますか？　　　Are you in any clubs?

Unit 03 Let me introduce a new member to you.

文法 ▶ 一般動詞（過去形）

ロブはミナコに友人のジャスティンを紹介します。会話では、人を紹介したり、確信を示したりする際の表現を学びます。また、文法では**一般動詞（過去形）**、読解では**単位 1（長さ）**に焦点を当てて学習します。

Warm-up

授業前に確認しておこう！

:. Vocabulary Preview

 1-14

1～10 の語句の意味として適切なものを a ～ j の中から選びましょう。

1. same	＿＿＿＿	a. 学科
2. experiment	＿＿＿＿	b. 卒業する
3. at first	＿＿＿＿	c. 男、（複数形で男女問わず）人たち
4. difficulty	＿＿＿＿	d. 大多数、大半
5. guy	＿＿＿＿	e. 同じ
6. major in	＿＿＿＿	f. 困難
7. distance	＿＿＿＿	g. 実験
8. department	＿＿＿＿	h. 距離
9. majority	＿＿＿＿	i. 最初は、初めは
10. graduate	＿＿＿＿	j. ～を専攻する

ビートに乗って 1～10 の語句を発音してみましょう。

:. Grammar Point : 一般動詞（過去形）

I <u>joined</u> the mathematics club yesterday.　（私は昨日、数学クラブに入部しました）
Justin <u>grew</u> up in Ohio.　（ジャスティンはオハイオで育ちました）

　過去の状況や行為・出来事を示す場合、**過去形**を用います。一般動詞を過去形にする場合には語尾に -ed をつけます。ただし、不規則に変化するものも多いので注意が必要です。巻末資料を参考にしながら下の表の空欄に適切な動詞の過去形を書き入れ確認しましょう。

1. ほとんどの動詞		語尾に -ed をつける	help　→ helped	listen → listened
2. -e で終わる動詞		語尾に -d をつける	use　→ used	like　→
3. y で終わる動詞	母音字 +y の場合	語尾に -ed をつける	enjoy → enjoyed	play　→
	子音字 +y の場合	y を i に変えて -ed をつける	study → studied	carry →
4. 母音字 1 つ + 子音字 1 つで終わる動詞*		語尾の子音を重ねて -ed をつける	plan　→ planned	stop　→
5. 例外的な動詞		不規則な変化をする	have → had	write →

＊厳密には、visit や remember、listen のように、最後の音節が強く発音されないものは子音字を重ねません。

一般動詞を使った過去形の文を否定文にするときは、動詞のすぐ前に didn't (=did not) をつけます。また疑問文にするには文の始めに did を持ってきます。いずれの場合も動詞は原形に戻します。下の例文の日本語訳を完成させながら確認しましょう。

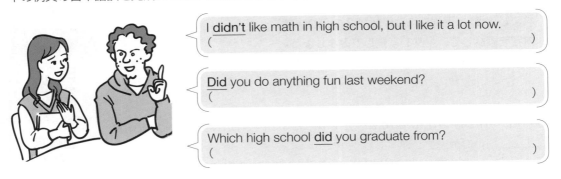

I **didn't** like math in high school, but I like it a lot now.
(　　　　　　　　　　　　　　　　　　　　　　　　)

Did you do anything fun last weekend?
(　　　　　　　　　　　　　　　　　　　　　　　　)

Which high school **did** you graduate from?
(　　　　　　　　　　　　　　　　　　　　　　　　)

　また、過去形で表される内容は、下記の表や図のように、<u>現在とはつながりがない</u>のがポイントです。下の例文の日本語訳を完成させながら確認しましょう。

過去の状態	I wanted to become a scientist when I was little. (　　　　)	過去　　現在
過去の１回きりの行為・出来事	My family went on a trip to Sydney last winter. (　　　　)	過去　　現在
過去の習慣や反復的行為	My father often went abroad on business. (　　　　)	過去　　現在

「その時〜していた」のように、過去に一時的に続いていた行為を表す場合は**過去進行形**(Unit 4)を用います。

 Let's Listen!　　　　　　　　　　　　　会話の大意を聞き取ろう！

ロブ、ミナコ、ジャスティンの会話を聞いて、質問に対する答えとして最も適切なものを（A）〜（C）の中から１つ選びましょう。　　　 1-15

Question 1　　Which statement is true of Justin?

(A) His last name is Guy.
(B) He met Minako yesterday.
(C) He's a member of the mathematics club.

Question 2　　What is Justin's major?

(A) Computer science
(B) Earth science
(C) Mathematics

Question 3　　What does Justin say about the club?

(A) The members are very kind.
(B) He helped the members a lot.
(C) There are eight members in the club.

Let's Check & Read Aloud!   音読してみよう！

1. スクリプトを見ながら会話をもう1度聞き、下線部に当てはまる表現を書き入れましょう。（下線部には単語が2つ入ります） 1-15
2. 内容を確認して、全文を音読してみましょう。
3. ロブ、ミナコ、ジャスティンの役割を3人のグループで演じてみましょう。

Let's Practice the Roleplay!

Rob's Role

Justin's Role

Minako's Role

Rob introduces Minako to his friend, Justin at the student lounge.

Rob　Hi, Justin. Have you guys met? Minako's going to join the club.

Justin　No, I ①_____ so. Hi, I'm Justin.

Minako　Hi, Justin. I'm Minako.

Justin　So, ②_____ the mathematics club.

Rob　Justin is also from Kent State* like me.

Justin　Yeah, that's right. I ③_____ earth science. How about you, Minako?

Minako　Me, too. We're all in the ④_____ .

Justin　That's great. Rob and I ⑤_____ eight months ago. At first everything was new to us, and we had ⑥_____ . But members of this club ⑦_____ a lot. They're very kind.

Rob　Yeah. I'm sure you'll have a ⑧_____ in this club, Minako.

Minako　Thanks. I'm sure I will.

[Note] ＊＝ Kent State University（ケント州立大学）

💡 **聞き取りのヒント**

great time は「グレイト・タイム」ではなく「グレイッタイム」のように聞こえます。このように同じ子音が連続する場合、同じ音が繰り返されるのではなく、前の子音が発音されず、その音が聞こえなくなりますので注意しましょう。また、聞き取りのヒントは音読のヒントでもあります。音読する際にも気をつけましょう。

 # Grammar

A. 例にならい、枠の中から適切な単語を選び、必要な場合は適切な形にして次の 1 ～ 4 の文を完成させましょう。

例 Rob and I (*came*) here eight months ago.

| come ✓ |
| rise |
| buy |
| sleep |
| conduct |

1. I (　　　　　　) well last night, so I feel much better today.

2. Justin (　　　　　　) a jacket yesterday. He likes it very much.

3. We (　　　　　　) an interesting experiment in science class last week.

4. The sun (　　　　　　) in the east and sets in the west.

B. 例にならい、カッコ内の動詞を肯定もしくは否定のいずれか適切な形に変えて文を完成させましょう。

例 "Did you finish your homework?" "No, I *didn't have* enough time." (have)

1. I was late for school, so I _____ able to take the exam. (be)

2. "Did you come here by bus?" "No, my brother _____ me a ride." (give)

3. "Did you major in engineering?" "No, I _____ in law. (major)

4. I overslept and _____ the first period. (miss)

C. 日本語の意味に合うようにカッコ内の語句を並べ替え、英文を完成させましょう。ただし、文の始めにくる単語も小文字にしてあり、1 つ余分な語句が含まれています。

1. 父は大学生の時、土木工学を専攻していました。

(in / majored / engineering / civil / my father / majors) when he was in college.

_____

2. 何を専攻していますか？

(is / major / majored / what / your) ?

_____

3. 1 年生の時、生物学を取りましたか？

(when / take / did / were / biology / you) you were a freshman?

_____

4. 兄はケント州立大学を卒業しました。

My (graduated / to / Kent State / from / University / brother).

_____

次のパッセージを読み、その内容について 1〜3 の質問に答えましょう。 1-16

Miles, Yards, and Feet

In the metric system of measurement, the most common units of distance are millimeters, centimeters, meters, and kilometers. This system is used by a majority of the world, including Japan. But the U.S. is an <u>exception</u>. In the U.S., distances on roads are measured in miles, and shorter distances are measured in yards and feet. One mile is equal to 1,609 meters, one yard is equal to three feet or 0.9144 meters, and one foot is equal to 12 inches or 0.3048 meters. Why hasn't the U.S. adopted the metric system? The biggest reasons may be simply time and money.

---

1. The underlined word "exception" means something that _____ .

   (A) is powerful in a group

   (B) doesn't follow a general rule

   (C) is commonly used

2. According to the passage, a mile is _____ a kilometer.

   (A) longer than

   (B) shorter than

   (C) the same length as

3. Which sentence is true?

   (A) Japan and the U.S. use the same units of distance.

   (B) The U.S. doesn't use the metric system because changing systems would be costly and inconvenient.

   (C) Miles and yards are units of distance used in the metric system of measurement.

📖 **Notes**

metric system of measurement: メートル法

mile: マイル（長さの単位）　　　　　　yard: ヤード（長さの単位）

foot: フィート（長さの単位）　　　　　adopt: 採用する

Challenge Yourself!

Part I **Photographs**

（A）〜（C）の英文を聞き、写真の描写として最も適切なものを選びましょう。 1-17

1.

(A)　　　(B)　　　(C)

2.
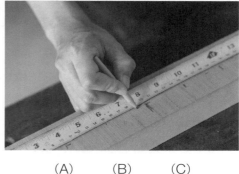

(A)　　　(B)　　　(C)

Part II **Question-Response**

最初に聞こえてくる英文に対する応答として最も適切なものを（A）〜（C）の中から選びましょう。 1-18

3.　（A）　　　（B）　　　（C）

4.　（A）　　　（B）　　　（C）

Part III **Short Conversations**

会話を聞き、下の英文が会話の内容と合っていれば T（True）、間違っていれば F（False）を○で囲みましょう。 1-19

5. Carlos made a good impression on the woman.　　　T　　　F

6. The man enjoys listening to his roommate's music.　　　T　　　F

 Let's Read Aloud & Write! 音読筆写で覚えよう！

授業のまとめとして、今日学習した対話文を3回書き写してしっかり覚えましょう。1度英文を声に出して読んでから書き写すと頭に残りやすくなります。

┤ **今日のまとめ** ├

英語で答えられますか？　　　Did you belong to any club in high school?

Unit 04 I'm looking for a part-time job.

文法 ▶ 進行形

学生ラウンジでミナコとジャスティンの話が続きます。会話では、詳細を尋ねたり、依頼したりする際の表現を学びます。また、また、文法では**進行形**、読解では**単位2（音の強さ）**に焦点を当てて学習します。

 **Warm-up**　　　　　　　授業前に確認しておこう！

Vocabulary Preview　　　　　　 1-20

1~10 の語句の意味として適切なものを a ~ j の中から選びましょう。

1. private	＿＿＿	a. （音の）大きさ
2. in fact	＿＿＿	b. 不平を言う
3. look for	＿＿＿	c. 実際には
4. work part-time	＿＿＿	d. （音などが）かすかな
5. inventor	＿＿＿	e. 通常の
6. tutor	＿＿＿	f. 個人用の
7. loudness	＿＿＿	g. ～を探す
8. faint	＿＿＿	h. 発明者
9. complain	＿＿＿	i. 家庭教師
10. normal	＿＿＿	j. アルバイトをする

ビートに乗って 1~10 の語句を発音してみましょう。

Grammar Point：進行形

I <u>work</u> part-time on weekends.	（私は週末にアルバイトをしています）[現在形]
I'm <u>working</u> right now.	（私は今、仕事中です）[現在進行形]
I <u>was working</u> at that time.	（私はその時、仕事中でした）[過去進行形]

　一般に現在形が普段の状態や動作を指すのに対し、今している最中の動作を表す場合には**現在進行形**を用い、≪ be 動詞 + 動詞の ing 形≫の形で表します。下の表の空欄に適切な動詞の形を書き入れて動詞の ing 形の作り方を確認しましょう。

1. ほとんどの動詞	語尾に ing をつける	sleep → sleeping	eat → eating
2. 子音 + -e で終わる動詞	語尾の e を取って ing をつける	give → giving	make →
3. -ie [ai] で終わる動詞	語尾の ie を y に変えて ing をつける	lie → lying	die →
4. 1 母音字 +1 子音字で終わる動詞	語尾の子音字を重ねて ing をつける	get → getting	stop →

過去形の be 動詞を使って**過去進行形**にすると「〜していた」という意味を表します。また、否定文にするときは be 動詞のすぐ後に not をつけ、疑問文にするには be 動詞を主語の前に持ってきます。下の例文の日本語訳を完成させながら使い方を確認しましょう。

I called you three times. What <u>were</u> you <u>doing</u>? <u>Were</u> you <u>sleeping</u>?
(　　　　　　　　　　　　　　　　　　　　　)

Sorry. I <u>wasn't sleeping</u>. I <u>was taking</u> an interview for a part-time job. And guess what? I got the job!
(　　　　　　　　　　　　　　　　　　　　　)

　進行形は「〜している」のように動作を表すものですから、know（知っている）などのように状態を表す動詞は通常、進行形にはなりません。ただし、have や live のように状態を表す動詞でも、次のような場合は進行形にすることができます。

We<u>'re having</u> dinner.　　　　　　　（私たちは晩御飯を食べているところです）
　　　　　　　　　　　　　　　　　　　＊この have は「〜を食べる」という意味

My sister <u>is living</u> in Seoul on business.　　（姉は仕事でソウルに住んでいます）
　　　＊ live は一般に「住んでいる」という状態を表しますが、進行形にすると「ずっとそこに住むわけではなく、一時的に住んでいる」という意味になります。

 ## Let's Listen!　　　　　　　　　　会話の大意を聞き取ろう！

ミナコとジャスティンの会話を聞いて、質問に対する答えとして最も適切なものを (A) 〜 (C) の中から 1 つ選びましょう。　　 1-21

Question 1 Does Justin work part-time?

(A) Yes, he started working last week.
(B) Yes, he works twice a week.
(C) No, he's looking for a job.

Question 2 Which sentence is true of Kenji?

(A) He learns English from Justin.
(B) He's not good at English.
(C) He teaches math to Minako.

Question 3 What does Minako ask Justin to do?

(A) Call her tonight
(B) Tell her Kenji's phone number
(C) Ask Kenji about a math class

Let's Check & Read Aloud!

音読してみよう！

1. スクリプトを見ながら会話をもう1度聞き、下線部に当てはまる表現を書き入れましょう。（下線部には単語が2つ入ります） 1-21
2. 内容を確認して、全文を音読してみましょう。
3. ミナコとジャスティンの役割をパートナーと一緒に演じてみましょう。

Let's Practice the Roleplay!

Minako's Role   Justin's Role

Minako and Justin continue to talk at the student lounge.

| Minako | I'm ①_____ a part-time job. Do you have one, Justin? |

| Justin | Oh, yes. I work as a ②_____ twice a week. I teach English to a high school student. |

| Minako | Do you work ③_____ ? |

| Justin | No, I only work on Monday and Thursday evenings. |

| Minako | Do you enjoy it? |

| Justin | Yes. My student is Kenji, and we enjoy ④_____ a lot of things. He speaks good English, but he often ⑤_____ he's not good at math. |

| Minako | Well, then, maybe I could ⑥_____ math? |

| Justin | Would you like to? Would you be interested in doing that? |

| Minako | Yes, I would. ⑦_____ ask him if he'd like a math class? |

| Justin | Sure. In fact, I'll ⑧_____ tonight. |

 **音読のヒント**

ウォーキングなど、カタカナ英語の影響もあって、talking など動詞の ing 形を「トーキング」のように「〜イング」と発音する人がいますが、ing の [iŋ] における [ŋ] は「ング」という感じの鼻にかけた音で、「グ」の音は鼻から出ていくため、はっきりとは聞こえない音です。「イン<u>グ</u>」ではなく、「イング」という感じです。

A. 例にならい、枠の中から適切な単語を選び、必要な場合は適切な形にして次の 1 ～ 4 の文を完成させましょう。

例 Turn down the television. We (*are studying*) now.

| study ✓ |
| know |
| feel |
| work |
| give |

1. I (   ) a presentation when you called me.

2. Rob (   ) as a private tutor every Monday. He enjoys his work.

3. Are you (   ) better now?

4. I (   ) Justin's phone number. Shall I call him?

B. 例にならい、次の英文をカッコ内の指示に従って書き換えましょう。

例 Charles works at a restaurant.(現在進行形に) *Charles is working at a restaurant.*

1. Justin doesn't look for a part-time job. （現在進行形に）
   _____

2. We had a great time at the welcome party for new members. （過去進行形に）
   _____

3. Do you save money to study abroad? （現在進行形に）
   _____

4. Did Minako give a presentation in English? （過去進行形に）
   _____

C. 日本語の意味に合うようにカッコ内の語句を並べ替え、英文を完成させましょう。ただし、文の始めにくる単語も小文字にしてあり、1 つ余分な語句が含まれています。

1. 彼らは科学部に所属しています。
   (the / science / to / they / belong / are belonging / club) .
   _____

2. 実験の準備をしているのですか？
   (preparing / the experiment / are / do / for / you) ?
   _____

3. その時は彼に数学を教えていました。
   (teaching / I / him / at / was / am / math) that time.
   _____

4. SDGs*についてはよく知っています。
   (lot / SDGs / I / know / a / am knowing / about) .
   _____

＊= Sustainable Development Goals （持続可能な開発目標）

Let's Read!

読解力を高めよう！

次のパッセージを読み、その内容について 1〜3 の質問に答えましょう。

 1-22

What Is a Decibel?

A decibel is a unit for measuring the loudness of sound. The word "decibel" is a combination of "deci" and "bel." "Deci" means one tenth of the stated unit, like "deciliter" and "decigram." The "bel" part honors Alexander Graham Bell, inventor of the telephone.

A "decibel" measures sounds in tenths of a "bel." You might need some examples to understand what that means. For example, a very faint sound, such as the sound of human breathing, is about 5 decibels, and normal conversation is usually around 60 decibels. ☐ someone shouts in your ear, the sound level may reach 100 decibels.

---

1. Which sentence is true?

   (A) A decibel is a unit for measuring the speed of sound.

   (B) The sound of human breathing is usually around 60 decibels.

   (C) The "bel" part in decibel was named after Alexander Graham Bell.

2. The word that belongs in the ☐ in this passage is ＿＿＿＿＿ .

   (A) If

   (B) Though

   (C) Because

3. What is the purpose of this passage?

   (A) To remember the life of Alexander Graham Bell

   (B) To explain how sound is measured

   (C) To give examples of a very faint sound

Notes

stated: 決められた　honor: 〜に敬意を払う

in tenths of: 〜の 10 分の 1 で　the word that belongs in the ☐: 空欄にあてはまる単語

Challenge Yourself!

Part I Photographs

(A)〜(C) の英文を聞き、写真の描写として最も適切なものを選びましょう。 1-23

1.

(A)   (B)   (C)

2.

(A)   (B)   (C)

Part II Question-Response

最初に聞こえてくる英文に対する応答として最も適切なものを（A）〜（C）の中から選びましょう。 1-24

3.   (A)   (B)   (C)

4.   (A)   (B)   (C)

Part III Short Conversations

会話を聞き、下の英文が会話の内容と合っていれば T（True）、間違っていれば F（False）を○で囲みましょう。 1-25

5. The man will have a class with the woman on the 15th.   T   F

6. The woman will have an interview for the job.   T   F

 Let's Read Aloud & Write!

授業のまとめとして、今日学習した対話文を3回書き写してしっかり覚えましょう。1度英文を声に出して読んでから書き写すと頭に残りやすくなります。

┤ **今日のまとめ** ├

英語で答えられますか？   Are you looking for a part-time job?

Unit 05

What are you going to do?

文法 ▶ 未来表現

部室でミナコとロブが話し合っています。会話では、予定を尋ねたり、驚きを示したりする際の表現を学びます。また、文法では**未来表現**、読解では**建築**に焦点を当てて学習します。

Warm-up

授業前に確認しておこう！

● Vocabulary Preview

🎵 1-26

1～10 の語句の意味として適切なものを a ～ j の中から選びましょう。

1. invention _____	a. 典型的な
2. have no idea _____	b. 実験室、研究所
3. annual _____	c. 表現
4. ethnic _____	d. 開催される
5. innovation _____	e.（展示会などで）ブースを出す
6. laboratory _____	f. 毎年の
7. take place _____	g. 民族の
8. typical _____	h. 革新、刷新
9. expression _____	i. 発明
10. run a booth _____	j. まったくわからない

ビートに乗って 1～10 の語句を発音してみましょう。

● Grammar Point : 未来表現

Hello, everyone. I'll take attendance now.

（みなさん、こんにちは。今から出席を取ります）

First, I'm going to talk about today's experiment.

（まず、今日の実験についてお話します）

　これから先のことを話す場合には、≪ will+ 動詞の原形≫や≪ be going to+ 動詞の原形≫といった形を使います。下の表で確認しましょう。

will	意志（～するつもりだ）	I'll join the science club.
	予測（～だろう）	Hurry up, or we'll be late for class.
be going to	計画や意志（～するつもりだ）	I'm going to explain the schedule for today.
	予測（～だろう）	Rob is going to be the next president of the mathematics club.

否定文にするときは、≪ will not ＋動詞の原形 ≫や≪ be not going to ＋動詞の原形 ≫のように、will や be 動詞のすぐ後に not をつけます。また、疑問文にするには will や be 動詞を主語の前に持ってきます。下の例文の日本語訳を完成させながら確認しましょう。

> won't = will not

I'm sorry I was late for class. It **won't** happen again.
(   )

What time **will** the experiment start?
(   )

Who **is going to** be the leader of the group?
(   )

　will と be going to はどちらもこれから先のことを表しますが、まったく同じ意味というわけではありません。**will は話をしている時点でそうすると決めたことを表すのに対し、be going to はすでに以前からそのつもりでいたことを表します。**次の例文でその違いを確認しておきましょう。

"If you have any questions, visit my office anytime.
（質問があればいつでも私の研究室を訪ねてください）

"Can I come during lunch break?"
（昼休みに行っても良いですか？）

"Sorry. **I'm going to** be out at that time."
（ごめんなさい。その時間は外出の予定です）

"I see. How about at three o'clock?"
（わかりました。3時ではどうでしょうか？）

"Sure. **I'll** be there."
（いいですよ。そこにいますから）

 Let's Listen!　　　　　　　　　　会話の大意を聞き取ろう！

ミナコとロブの会話を聞いて、質問に対する答えとして最も適切なものを（A）～（C）の中から1つ選びましょう。 1-27

Question 1　　What is Rob doing right now?

(A) Getting ready for a school event

(B) Eating a hamburger

(C) Preparing for an exam

Question 2　　What is true of the International Night?

(A) It takes place in June.

(B) It will take place next week.

(C) It takes place once a year.

Question 3　　What are Rob and Justin going to cook?

(A) Pumpkin pie

(B) Apple pie

(C) Pizza

Let's Check & Read Aloud!

音読してみよう！

1. スクリプトを見ながら会話をもう1度聞き、下線部に当てはまる表現を書き入 1-27
   れましょう。（下線部には単語が2つ入ります）
2. 内容を確認して、全文を音読してみましょう。
3. ミナコとロブの役割をパートナーと一緒に演じてみましょう。

Let's Practice the Roleplay!

Minako's Role   Rob's Role

Minako speaks to Rob at the clubroom.

Minako	Hi, Rob. ①_____ ?
Rob	Nothing much. I'm just ②_____ this year's International Night.
Minako	International Night? What's that?
Rob	It's ③_____ school event that takes place in July. You can try a lot of ethnic foods and ④_____ different cultures.
Minako	Sounds interesting. What are you going to do there?
Rob	Justin ⑤_____ are going to run a booth for American culture. ⑥_____ going to cook some American dishes.
Minako	What are you going to cook? Hamburgers?
Rob	Of course. But we're going to ⑦_____ apple pies, too.
Minako	Is apple pie a typical American food?
Rob	Yes, we have an expression "as American as apple pie."
Minako	Oh, really? I ⑧_____ idea.

💡 **音読のヒント**

「子音で終わる単語」の後に「母音で始まる単語」が続いた場合には、単語と単語がつながって聞こえることがあります。これを音の連結と言い、例えば an annual は「アン・アニュアル」ではなく「ア ナニュアル」のように聞こえます。音読する際は、モデル音声のように連結させて読むべきところは連結させて音読し、カタカナ英語の発音にならないようにしましょう。

Grammar

A. 例にならい、枠の中から適切な単語を選び、必要な場合は適切な形にして次の 1 〜 4 の文を完成させましょう。

> 例　Tomorrow is Minako's birthday. She'll (　*be*　) 19.

be ✓
give
enter
belong
come

1. We're going to (　　　　) a presentation tomorrow.

2. I (　　　　) to the science club when I was in high school.

3. I'll wait here until Rob (　　　　) back from the laboratory.

4. My brother will (　　　　) junior high school next year.

B. 例にならい、カッコ内から正しい語句を選び○で囲みましょう。

> 例　Hurry! (We won't /(We're going to)) be late for the experiment.

1. "How about studying in the library?" "Sorry. (I'll / I'm going to) visit my mother in the hospital."

2. "Is Minako coming to the International Night?" "I don't know. (I'll / I'm going to) ask her."

3. I'm sorry, Professor Oki. (I'm not / I won't) be late for class again.

4. I'll let you know the results of the experiment as soon as I (get / will get) them.

C. 日本語の意味に合うようにカッコ内の語句を並べ替え、英文を完成させましょう。ただし、文の始めにくる単語も小文字にしてあり、1 つ余分な語句が含まれています。

1. 放課後は何をする予定ですか？
   (are / will / what / to do / you / going) after school?

   _____

2. 後でそのプロジェクトを詳しく説明します。
   (in / I'll / I'm going / project / the / explain) detail later.

   _____

3. それはいつ準備が整いますか？
   (will / ready / going to / it / be / when) ?

   _____

4. 誰が数学クラブの部長になるでしょうか？
   (going to / going / who / be / is / the president) of the mathematics club?

   _____

次のパッセージを読み、その内容について 1〜3 の質問に答えましょう。   1-28

Architects

The word "architect"—from the Greek "arkhitekton"—means "master builder" or "chief creator." Architects are master designers, but their designs can't be built without suitable materials. Of all these materials, perhaps none is as important as concrete. Its use was pioneered by the Romans, who used it to build temples, theaters, and so on. The use of concrete was further improved in the 19th century, when it was <u>reinforced</u> with steel. This innovation, and the invention of the elevator, made possible our modern-day skyscrapers. Our 21st century buildings may stand tall, but their creators <u>stand on the shoulders of</u> giants, the "master builders" of the ancient world.

---

1. Which sentence is true?

   (A) The Romans pioneered the use of concrete.

   (B) The Romans began reinforcing concrete with steel in the 19th century.

   (C) Early Roman buildings were built by Greek architects.

2. The underlined word "reinforced" means made _____ .

   (A) stronger

   (B) heavier

   (C) higher

3. The underlined phrase "stand on the shoulders of" means _____ .

   (A) to benefit from the experience of

   (B) to be much better than

   (C) to be able to see more clearly than

📖 **Notes**

Greek: ギリシャ語の   master: 熟練した

pioneer: 先駆けて〜を開発する   skyscraper: 超高層ビル

Challenge Yourself!

Part I Photographs

(A)〜(C) の英文を聞き、写真の描写として最も適切なものを選びましょう。 1-29

1.

(A) (B) (C)

2.

(A) (B) (C)

Part II Question-Response

最初に聞こえてくる英文に対する応答として最も適切なものを（A)〜(C) の中 1-30
から選びましょう。

3. (A) (B) (C)

4. (A) (B) (C)

Part III Short Conversations

会話を聞き、下の英文が会話の内容と合っていれば T（True)、間違っていれば 1-31
F（False）を○で囲みましょう。

5. The woman tells the man that she's a vegetarian.   T   F

6. The wrong date is on the poster.   T   F

 # Let's Read Aloud & Write!

音読筆写で覚えよう！

授業のまとめとして、今日学習した対話文を３回書き写して
しっかり覚えましょう。１度英文を声に出して読んでから書き
写すと頭に残りやすくなります。

今日のまとめ

英語で答えられますか？   What are you going to do this weekend?

Unit 06 Could you take a look at this slide?

プレゼンを控えたミナコは、プレゼンで使うスライドについてジャスティンに相談をします。会話では、状況を説明したり、助言をしたりする際の表現を学びます。また、文法では助動詞、読解ではグラフ1（円グラフ）に焦点を当てて学習します。

Warm-up

授業前に確認しておこう！

Vocabulary Preview

CD 1-32

1〜10 の語句の意味として適切なものを a〜j の中から選びましょう。

1. pie chart	_____	a. 全体
2. bar graph	_____	b. 〜を修正する
3. compare	_____	c. 適した
4. submit	_____	d. （〜より）むしろ
5. instead of	_____	e. 円グラフ
6. right away	_____	f. 〜の代わりに
7. whole	_____	g. すぐに
8. suited	_____	h. 比較する
9. rather	_____	i. 提出する
10. revise	_____	j. 棒グラフ

ビートに乗って 1〜10 の語句を発音してみましょう。

Grammar Point : 助動詞

You <u>must</u> be tired.　（きっとお疲れでしょう）

<u>Can</u> I be excused*?

　　　　　（席を外してもよろしいでしょうか？／お手洗いに行ってもいいですか？）

＊ excuse は「退出を許す」という意味で、直訳は「私は席を外すことを許されますか？」となります。

<u>助動詞</u>は動詞の前につけて動詞に意味を追加するものです。助動詞の場合、一般動詞と違って主語が 3 人称単数であっても語尾に -s や -es がつくことはありません。

主な助動詞とその用法は下の表の通りです。

can	〜できる（be able to） 〜してもよい	must	〜しなければならない（have to） 〜に違いない
may	〜してもよい 〜かもしれない	might	〜かもしれない
should	〜すべきである 〜のはずである	used to	以前は〜だった

must の否定形 must not は「～してはいけない」という意味になり、「～する必要はない」と言いたい場合は don't have to を使います。また、would と could はそれぞれ助動詞 will と can の過去形ですが、実際のコミュニケーションにおいては過去の意味で使うのではなく、丁寧な言い方をする場合によく用いられます。

would like	～をいただきたいのですが	＊ want や want to よりも丁寧で控えめな感じがします。	
would like to	～したいのですが		
Would you ...?	～していただけないでしょうか？	＊ Will you ...? や Can you ...? よりも丁寧で控えめな感じがします。	
Could you ...?			

上の表を参考にして、下の例文の日本語訳を完成させましょう。

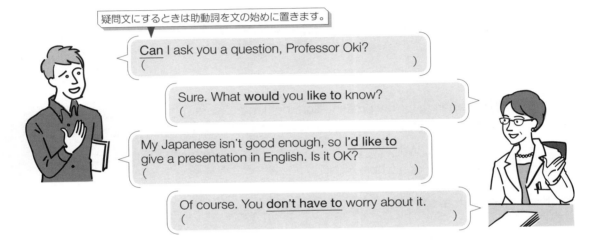

疑問文にするときは助動詞を文の始めに置きます。

Can I ask you a question, Professor Oki?
(   )

Sure. What would you like to know?
(   )

My Japanese isn't good enough, so I'd like to give a presentation in English. Is it OK?
(   )

Of course. You don't have to worry about it.
(   )

 Let's Listen!

会話の大意を聞き取ろう！

ミナコとジャスティンの会話を聞いて、質問に対する答えとして最も適切なものを(A) ～（C）の中から1つ選びましょう。 1-33

Question 1 What does Minako ask Justin to do?

(A) Make slides for her presentation
(B) Check the slide
(C) Give a presentation

Question 2 What is Justin's advice?

(A) Use a bar graph
(B) Use more animations
(C) Use a pie chart

Question 3 What will Minako probably do next?

(A) Make some changes to the slide
(B) Get more information
(C) Ask someone for help

Let's Check & Read Aloud!

1. スクリプトを見ながら会話をもう１度聞き、下線部に当てはまる表現を書き入れましょう。（下線部には単語が２つ入ります） 1-33

2. 内容を確認して、全文を音読してみましょう。

3. ミナコとジャスティンの役割をパートナーと一緒に演じてみましょう。

Let's Practice the Roleplay!

Minako's Role   Justin's Role

Minako speaks to Justin at the clubroom.

Minako	Excuse me, but can I talk to you for a minute?
Justin	Sure. What's up?
Minako	I'm preparing for my presentation, but I'm not sure ①_____ of graph I should use. Could you take a look at this slide?
Justin	No problem. Well, ②_____ . You're trying to ③_____ _____ of a whole, right?
Minako	Yeah, that's right.
Justin	Then, it ④_____ better to use a pie chart instead of a bar graph.
Minako	Hmm, you're right. Pie charts are ⑤_____ . That's for sure. Any other comments?
Justin	I think you ⑥_____ much information on the slide. Why don't you use keywords ⑦_____ sentences?
Minako	Yeah, thanks. I see what you mean. ⑧_____ the slide right away.

 音読のヒント

カタカナ英語の影響で presentation や information を「プレゼンテーション」、「インフォメーション」のように発音していませんか？　特に、カタカナ英語で長音符（ー）を使っている箇所は実際の英語の発音ではそうならない場合が多いので注意しましょう。正しくは、それぞれ「プリゼンテイション」[prìːzentéiʃən]、「インフォメイション」[ìnfərméiʃən] です。

 **Grammar**　　　　　　　　　　　　　　　文法に強くなろう！

A. 例にならい、枠の中から適切な単語を選び、必要な場合は適切な形にして次の 1 ～ 4 の文を完成させましょう。

> 例 (May) I be excused?

| used to |
| could |
| may ✓ |
| shall |
| have to |

1. Let's study for the exam together, (　　　　　) we?

2. Sorry, I can't talk now. I (　　　　　) get to class.

3. (　　　　　) you take a look at my report?

4. My daughter (　　　　　) hate math, but now she enjoys it.

B. 例にならい、カッコ内から正しい語句を選び○で囲みましょう。

> 例 I don't believe it. It (can /(can't)) be true.

1. "(Could I / Could you) ask you a favor?" "Sure. How can I help you?"

2. (Would you like / Would you like to) join our research group?

3. (I'd like / I'd like to) your feedback on my presentation.

4. (Shall we / Shall you) prepare a presentation later?

C. 日本語の意味に合うようにカッコ内の語句を並べ替え、英文を完成させましょう。ただし、文の始めにくる単語も小文字にしてあり、1 つ余分な語句が含まれています。

1. レポートは今日提出しなければなりませんか？

(have to / do / the / submit / I / must) report today?

_____

2. 棒グラフを使うほうが良いかもしれません。

(better / might / is / be / to / it) use a bar graph.

_____

3. あそこにはかつて大きな工場がありました。

There (to / be / used / was / a / big) factory over there.

_____

4. 日本語でプレゼンをする必要はありません。

You (a presentation / have / mustn't / give / don't / to) in Japanese.

_____

Let's Read!

次のパッセージを読み、その内容について 1〜3 の質問に答えましょう。　 1-34

What Is a Pie Chart?

A pie chart is a type of graph that represents the data in a circular graph. It is also known as a "circle chart." Here, the terms "pie" and "slices" represent the whole and the parts of the whole, respectively, and the slices of pie show the relative size of the data. Pie charts are probably better than any other visual for expressing a part-to-whole relationship. If you want your audience to have a general sense of the part-to-whole relationship in your data, a pie chart could meet your needs. It is best used with small datasets, and it should not be used for comparing the precise sizes of the slices.

---

1. Which sentence is true?

   (A) Pie charts make it easy for us to compare data in great detail.

   (B) Pie charts are most effective when using a small dataset.

   (C) Pie charts make it possible to visualize data in columns.

2. According to the passage, "slices" represent _____ .

   (A) the whole

   (B) circles

   (C) parts of the whole

3. The underlined word "precise" means _____ .

   (A) exact

   (B) rough

   (C) final

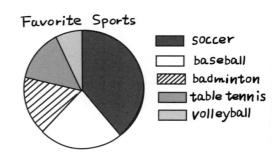

Favorite Sports

- soccer
- baseball
- badminton
- table tennis
- volleyball

 Notes

term: 用語　　　respectively: それぞれ　　　relative: 相対的な

Challenge Yourself!

Part I Photographs

（A）〜（C）の英文を聞き、写真の描写として最も適切なものを選びましょう。

 1-35

1.

（A）　　　（B）　　　（C）

2.

（A）　　　（B）　　　（C）

Part II Question-Response

最初に聞こえてくる英文に対する応答として最も適切なものを（A）〜（C）の中から選びましょう。

 1-36

3.　（A）　　　（B）　　　（C）

4.　（A）　　　（B）　　　（C）

Part III Short Conversations

会話を聞き、下の英文が会話の内容と合っていれば T（True）、間違っていれば F（False）を○で囲みましょう。

 1-37

5. The woman suggests adding more sentences to the slides.　　　T　　　F

6. The man and woman agree to use a bar graph.　　　T　　　F

 Let's Read Aloud & Write!

授業のまとめとして、今日学習した対話文を３回書き写してしっかり覚えましょう。１度英文を声に出して読んでから書き写すと頭に残りやすくなります。

┤ **今日のまとめ** ├

英語で答えられますか？　　　Are you good at giving presentations?

Unit 07 I'm so frustrated.

ジャスティンはミナコが夜遅くまで部室でパソコンに向かっているのを見つけ、話しかけます。会話では、感謝したり、お礼への返答をしたりする際の表現を学びます。また、文法では**受動態**、読解では**グラフ2（棒グラフ）**に焦点を当てて学習します。

Warm-up

授業前に確認しておこう！

⋮ Vocabulary Preview

🎵 1-38

1〜10の語句の意味として適切なものを a 〜 j の中から選びましょう。

1. frustrate ＿＿＿＿　　　a.（表計算ソフトの）セル、升目
2. sum ＿＿＿＿　　　b. 〜を口にする、〜に言及する
3. empty ＿＿＿＿　　　c. 〜をイライラさせる
4. cell ＿＿＿＿　　　d. 〜を解決する、〜を直す
5. column ＿＿＿＿　　　e. かなり、非常に
6. enter ＿＿＿＿　　　f. 値
7. mention ＿＿＿＿　　　g.（パソコンにデータなど）を入力する
8. quite ＿＿＿＿　　　h.（数や量の）合計
9. value ＿＿＿＿　　　i.（表などの）縦の列
10. fix ＿＿＿＿　　　j. 空の

ビートに乗って 1〜10 の語句を発音してみましょう。

⋮ Grammar Point：受動態

Rob <u>made</u> our club's website.

（ロブが私たちのクラブのホームページを作りました）［能動態］

Our club's website <u>was made</u> by Rob.

（私たちのクラブのホームページはロブによって作られました）［受動態］

> 「〜によって」は by で表しますが、誰がしたのかが重要でない場合には不要です。

　「〜は…される／されている」のように、何らかの動作を受ける意味を表す場合には、**受動態**を用い、≪ be 動詞＋過去分詞≫という形で表します。これに対して、これまで学習してきた「〜は…する」のように、何かに働きかける意味を表す文を**能動態**と言います。

　能動態にするか受動態にするかは、話題になっている「もの」や「こと」によって決まります。次の例文では、話題が「科学プロジェクト」なので受動態が使われているわけです。

　Our school has started a new science project. It<u>'s called</u> Galaxy Project.

　（私たちの学校は新しい科学プロジェクトを始めました。それはギャラクシー・プロジェクトという名前です）

この例文は "We call it Galaxy Project." のように能動態で表現することも可能ですが、受動態で表現する方が自然です。また、過去分詞は、start → started（過去形）→ started（過去分詞）のように、多くの場合動詞の過去形と同じ形ですが、begin → began（過去形）→ begun（過去分詞）のように不規則に変化するものもあります。巻末資料を参考にしながら下の表の空欄に適切な動詞の形を書き入れ確認しましょう。

不規則動詞の変化パターン	原形	過去形	過去分詞
A-A-A （原形、過去形、過去分詞がすべて同じ）	cost put	cost	cost
A-B-A （原形と過去分詞が同じ）	become run		
A-B-B （過去形と過去分詞が同じ）	bring meet		
A-B-C （原形、過去形、過去分詞がすべて異なる）	speak write		

受動態にも能動態と同じように、過去形や未来表現、進行形などがあります。下の例文の日本語訳を完成させながら使い方を確認しましょう。

> 過去形は≪ was/were + 過去分詞≫となります。

All the presentations **were given** in English.
(   )

> 進行形は≪ be 動詞 +being+ 過去分詞≫となります。

My laptop **is being repaired**.
(   )

> 未来表現は≪ will be+ 過去分詞≫や≪ be going to be+ 過去分詞≫を使います。

It **will be sent** back to me after it's repaired.
(   )

 Let's Listen!　　　　　　　　　　　　　会話の大意を聞き取ろう！

ミナコとジャスティンの会話を聞いて、質問に対する答えとして最も適切なものを
(A) 〜 (C) の中から１つ選びましょう。　　　　　　　　　　 1-39

Question 1 According to Minako, what is the problem with her computer?

(A) It makes a strange noise.

(B) It keeps freezing.

(C) It keeps sending a warning.

Question 2 Was Justin able to fix her problem?

(A) Yes, he says it was quite simple.

(B) Yes, he says it was very difficult.

(C) No, he says it's impossible.

Question 3 What will Minako probably do next?

(A) Go to dinner with him

(B) Go home

(C) Go to a computer repair shop

Let's Check & Read Aloud!

音読してみよう！

1. スクリプトを見ながら会話をもう1度聞き、下線部に当てはまる表現を書き入れましょう。（下線部には単語が2つ入ります） 1-39

2. 内容を確認して、全文を音読してみましょう。

3. ミナコとジャスティンの役割をパートナーと一緒に演じてみましょう。

Let's Practice the Roleplay!

Justin's Role   Minako's Role

Justin finds Minako at the clubroom and speaks to her.

Justin: Oh, Minako! Are you still working on your presentation? It's already eight o'clock!

Minako: I'm afraid so. I'm not ①＿＿＿＿＿＿＿ making graphs. Every time I enter the data, I get the ②＿＿＿＿＿＿＿ message. I'm so frustrated.

Justin: That's too bad. What does the error message say?

Minako: It says #VALUE![1]

Justin: I see. Well, then, let me just take a ③＿＿＿＿＿＿＿ it.

Minako: Oh, that's very ④＿＿＿＿＿＿＿ you.

After a while

Justin: All right. Here we go. I think the problem ⑤＿＿＿＿＿＿＿ .

Minako: Wow! How did you do that?

Justin: Well, it's ⑥＿＿＿＿＿＿＿ . This "Sum" column was referring to[2] ⑦＿＿＿＿＿＿＿ . Excel[3] can't calculate the sum of empty columns, so it was giving you an error.

Minako: Oh, thank you very much. Now I can go home and relax.

Justin: Don't ⑧＿＿＿＿＿＿＿ . I'm glad I could help.

[Notes] 1. #VALUE!: エクセルのエラーメッセージの一つで、「入力した数式に問題があるか、参照先のセルに問題がある」ことを示す。 2. refer to: 〜を参照する 3. Excel: エクセル（マイクロソフト社が販売している表計算ソフト名）

 **音読のヒント**

単語の最後にくる l [l] は、つづり字からつい「ル」に近い音を予想しますが、実際には「ゥ」のように聞こえます。例えば、well [wél] は「ウェル」ではなく、むしろ「ウェゥ」のように聞こえます。well は、「上手に、十分に」という副詞だけでなく、「ええと、そうですね、さて」という間投詞としても使われますが、この場合は話のつなぎということを意識して発音すると良いでしょう。

Grammar

A. 例にならい、枠の中から適切な単語を選び、必要な場合は適切な形にして次の 1 ～ 4 の文を完成させましょう。

例　Paper (*is made*) from wood.

invite
hold
make ✓
submit
build

1. I (　　　　　) to the research group, but I didn't join it.

2. This laboratory (　　　　　) five years ago.

3. A welcome party for new members will (　　　　　) this weekend.

4. You need to (　　　　　) your report by tomorrow.

B. 例にならい、カッコ内から正しい語句を選び○で囲みましょう。

例　This new science project (calls / is called) Galaxy Project.

1. Some volunteers (helped / were helped) the project.

2. The experiment will (last / be lasted) for a few hours.

3. My computer is (been / being) repaired now.

4. Professor Cooper is known (by / for) his work in biology.

C. 日本語の意味に合うようにカッコ内の語句を並べ替え、英文を完成させましょう。ただし、文の始めにくる単語も小文字にしてあり、1 つ余分な語句が含まれています。

1. この表計算ソフトは世界中で使われています。
   This spreadsheet (using / software / used / the world / around / is) .

   _____

2. 私はプレゼン資料をたくさん準備しました。
   (prepared / preparing / presentation / I / materials / a lot of) .

   _____

3. プレゼンは英語でされなければなりません。
   (the / are / given / be / must / presentations) in English.

   _____

4. 大雨のため、全授業が休講になりました。
   (was / canceled / to / due / were / all the classes) heavy rain.

   _____

次のパッセージを読み、その内容について 1〜3 の質問に答えましょう。 1-40

What Is a Bar Chart?

A bar chart is a graph with <u>rectangular</u> bars. It has an x-axis and a y-axis. In many cases, the x-axis runs horizontally (flat) and represents the categories, while the y-axis runs vertically (up and down) and represents a value for those categories. In the graph below, the values are percentages.

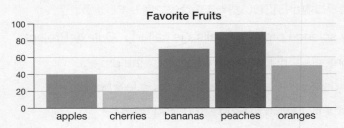

Favorite Fruits

Bar charts, also known as bar graphs, are used to compare things between different groups. [____], it's easier to see which item is the most popular by glancing at the above chart rather than looking at a line of numbers. They can also show changes over time, or reveal patterns in periodic sequences.

---

1. The underlined word "rectangular" describes the _____ of the bars.

   (A) shape

   (B) color

   (C) percentage

2. The word or phrase that belongs in the [____] in this passage is _____ .

   (A) As a result

   (B) However

   (C) For example

3. Which sentence is true?

   (A) Bar charts are completely different from bar graphs.

   (B) Bar charts can be used to show changes over time.

   (C) In many cases, the y-axis represents the categories.

📖 **Notes**

axis: 軸　　glance: ちらっと見る　　periodic sequence: 周期的な配列

Challenge Yourself!

Part I ▸ Photographs

(A)～(C) の英文を聞き、写真の描写として最も適切なものを選びましょう。　🎧 1-41

1.

(A)　　　(B)　　　(C)

2.
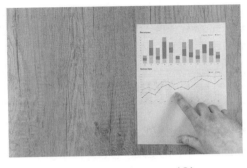
(A)　　　(B)　　　(C)

Part II ▸ Question-Response

最初に聞こえてくる英文に対する応答として最も適切なものを（A）～（C）の中から選びましょう。　🎧 1-42

3.　(A)　　　(B)　　　(C)

4.　(A)　　　(B)　　　(C)

Part III ▸ Short Conversations

会話を聞き、下の英文が会話の内容と合っていれば T（True）、間違っていれば F（False）を○で囲みましょう。　🎧 1-43

5. The man has a problem but solves it by himself.　　　T　　　F

6. The man decides to use a macro in his slides.　　　T　　　F

 # Let's Read Aloud & Write!

授業のまとめとして、今日学習した対話文を 3 回書き写してしっかり覚えましょう。1 度英文を声に出して読んでから書き写すと頭に残りやすくなります。

┤ 今日のまとめ ├

英語で答えられますか？　　Do you often make graphs in Excel?

Unit 08 It's something we need to think about.

文法 ▶ 現在完了形

学生食堂でミナコはジャスティンに情報倫理の授業について尋ねます。会話では、経験を尋ねたり、可能性を示したりする際の表現を学びます。また、文法では**現在完了形**、読解では<u>人体1（骨）</u>に焦点を当てて学習します。

Warm-up

授業前に確認しておこう！

Vocabulary Preview

1-44

1〜10の語句の意味として適切なものを a 〜 j の中から選びましょう。

1. ethics	＿＿＿＿	a. 評価する
2. sign up	＿＿＿＿	b. 〜に焦点を当てる
3. technology	＿＿＿＿	c. 倫理
4. advance	＿＿＿＿	d. 推薦する
5. artificial	＿＿＿＿	e. まったくそのとおり
6. intelligence	＿＿＿＿	f. 進歩、進歩する
7. focus on	＿＿＿＿	g. 登録する
8. absolutely	＿＿＿＿	h. 知能
9. recommend	＿＿＿＿	i. 人工の
10. evaluate	＿＿＿＿	j. 科学技術

ビートに乗って1〜10の語句を発音してみましょう。

Grammar Point : 現在完了形

I've *already* <u>handed</u> in the report, so I can relax today.

（私はすでにレポートを提出したので、今日はゆっくりできます）

> 否定文にするには have/has の後に not をつけます。また、会話では短縮形がよく使われます。

I <u>haven't taken</u> the subject *yet*. （私はまだその科目を取っていません）
<u>Have</u> you <u>taken</u> the subject *yet*? （もうその科目を取ってしまいましたか？）

> 疑問文にするには have/has を主語の前に持ってきます。

　過去にしたことや過去に起こったことを現在と結びつけて話す場合には**現在完了形**を用い、《 have/has+ 過去分詞》という形で表します。主語が he など3人称単数の場合は have ではなく has を使います。現在完了形は、現在の状況を述べる言い方なので、last month など、明確に過去の時点を表す表現とは一緒に使いません。次の表で過去形との違いを確認しましょう。

現在完了形（I've broken my arm.）	過去形（I broke my arm.）
今も骨折している	今は治っているのかどうか不明

　また、現在完了形の表す意味にはいくつか種類があり、just（ちょうど今）やalready（すでに）、yet（もうすでに、まだ）などの副詞が意味を見極める上でのポイントになります。次の表の例文の日本語訳を完成させながらそれぞれの意味を確認しましょう。

完了	～してしまった	"Have you taken your medicine *yet*?" "Yes. I took it after breakfast." (　　　　　　　　　　　　　　　　　　　　　　　　　)
	～したところだ	"Have you taken your medicine *yet*?" "Yes. I've *just* taken it." (　　　　　　　　　　　　　　　　　　　　　　　　　)
経験	～したことがある	Have you *ever* done any fieldwork? (　　　　　　　　　　　　　　　　　　　　　　　　　)
継続	ずっと～している	Rob has been in the hospital for a month. (　　　　　　　　　　　　　　　　　　　　　　　　　)

 ## Let's Listen!　　　　　　　　　会話の大意を聞き取ろう！

ミナコとジャスティンの会話を聞いて、質問に対する答えとして最も適切なものを　 1-45
(A) ～ (C) の中から1つ選びましょう。

Question 1　What is true of the Ethics and I.T. course?

(A) Minako is taking it this year.
(B) Justin took it last year.
(C) Justin is taking it this year.

Question 2　According to Minako, what type of technology is moving very fast?

(A) Communication technology
(B) Education technology
(C) Medical technology

Question 3　What will Minako probably do tomorrow?

(A) Sign up for the course
(B) Recommend the course to her friends
(C) Ask the teacher about the course

Let's Check & Read Aloud!

音読してみよう！

1. スクリプトを見ながら会話をもう１度聞き、下線部に当てはまる表現を書き入れましょう。（下線部には単語が２つ入ります） 1-45

2. 内容を確認して、全文を音読してみましょう。

3. ミナコとジャスティンの役割をパートナーと一緒に演じてみましょう。

Let's Practice the Roleplay!

Minako's Role   Justin's Role

Minako and Justin are talking in the school cafeteria.

Minako Justin, I was wondering if ① _____ this course, Ethics and I.T.[1]

Justin Yes, I took it last year. It was really interesting. Have you ② _____ _____ already?

Minako Not yet. But now I think I might. It's something we need to ③ _____ _____ , right?

Justin Yeah, ④ _____ so quickly, but our ethical frameworks[2] can't keep up.

Minako I know. I heard that advances in medical technology happen so fast that doctors don't have enough time to ⑤ _____ .

Justin And with artificial intelligence, the challenges are going to be ⑥ _____ _____ . We need to think about these things.

Minako So you'd recommend that I take the course?

Justin Absolutely. ⑦ _____ just focus on progress.

Minako I'll sign up tomorrow.

Justin Great. I'm so glad you ⑧ _____ .

[Notes] 1.= information technology 情報技術 2. 倫理的枠組み

 **音読のヒント**

"I heard that advances in medical technology ...." で使われている接続詞の that は、「〜だと聞きました」の「と」に当たる表現ですから、読む際には弱く「ザット」[ðət] と発音します。また、ポーズを取るときはその前で取ります。例えば、"I think that it's too difficult." という文を読む際にどこかで息つぎをするとすれば、I think と that の間となります。実際には I think that の後で切ることもありますが、その場合は次に何を言おうか言葉に詰まって考えているときです。

Grammar

A. 例にならい、枠の中から適切な単語を選び、必要な場合は適切な形にして次の 1 〜 4 の文を完成させましょう。

例　How long have you (*felt*) this way?

take
be
hand
go
feel ✓

1. My mother has (　　　　　) in the hospital for a month.

2. I (　　　　　) the PCR test yesterday, and I tested negative.

3. I (　　　　　) to the dentist two days ago.

4. Have you (　　　　　) in your report yet?

B. 例にならい、カッコ内から正しい語句を選び○で囲みましょう。

例　I've had a toothache (since /(for)) a week.

1. When (did you take / have you taken) the medicine?

2. My wife (took / has taken) an eye exam yesterday.

3. Minako has had a high fever (since / for) a few days ago.

4. I haven't gotten a blood test (already / yet).

C. 日本語の意味に合うようにカッコ内の語句を並べ替え、英文を完成させましょう。ただし、文の始めにくる単語も小文字にしてあり、1 つ余分な語句が含まれています。

1. 今までにフィールドワークをしたことがありますか？
(fieldwork / ever did / have / any / you / ever done) ?

_____

2. 昨日の夜、薬を飲みました。
(have taken / last / took / medicine / I / some) night.

_____

3. 健康診断を受けたところです。
(medical / having / had / checkup / a / I've just).

_____

4. 階段から落ちた時、右手を骨折しました。
(right arm / I / broke / have broken / my / when) I fell down the stairs.

_____

Let's Read!

次のパッセージを読み、その内容について 1〜3 の質問に答えましょう。

 1-46

Bones

Every person has a skeleton made up of so many bones. These include the bones of the skull, spine, ribs, arms and legs. Bones are hard and they support our whole body. If we didn't have bones, our body would be like a jellyfish. Bones work with muscles and joints to hold our body together and support freedom of movement. They also protect delicate internal organs, such as the brain, heart and lungs. How many bones are there in our body? The adult human body has 206 bones and a baby has about 300 bones. As the baby grows, some of its bones fuse together to form bigger bones.

---

1. The underlined word "skull" means a bone that protects our _____ .

   (A) brain

   (B) heart

   (C) stomach

2. The underlined phrase "internal organs" means the parts of your body that _____ .

   (A) help you to see, eat and walk

   (B) carry out a particular function within your body

   (C) protect the bones and skeleton

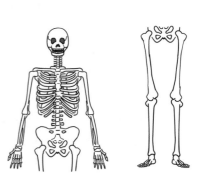

3. Which sentence is true?

   (A) The adult human body has 300 bones.

   (B) A baby has fewer bones than an adult.

   (C) The bones in our bodies change after birth.

Notes

skeleton: 骨格   spine: 脊椎   rib: 肋骨、あばら骨   joint: 関節   fuse: 結合する

Challenge Yourself!

Part I **Photographs**

(A) ～ (C) の英文を聞き、写真の描写として最も適切なものを選びましょう。 1-47

1.
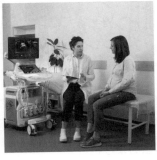

(A)　　　(B)　　　(C)

2.
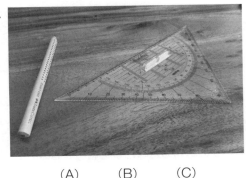

(A)　　　(B)　　　(C)

Part II **Question-Response**

最初に聞こえてくる英文に対する応答として最も適切なものを（A)～(C)の中から選びましょう。 1-48

3.　(A)　　　(B)　　　(C)

4.　(A)　　　(B)　　　(C)

Part III **Short Conversations**

会話を聞き、下の英文が会話の内容と合っていれば T（True）、間違っていれば F（False）を○で囲みましょう。 1-49

5. The woman was playing soccer when she cut her foot.　　　T　　　F

6. The man wasn't wearing any shoes when he broke his toe.　　　T　　　F

 Let's Read Aloud & Write!

授業のまとめとして、今日学習した対話文を３回書き写してしっかり覚えましょう。１度英文を声に出して読んでから書き写すと頭に残りやすくなります。

┤ **今日のまとめ** ├

英語で答えられますか？　　　Are you taking a course in ethics and I.T.?

Unit 09
I'm ready to start the experiment.

 **文法 ▶ 不定詞**

ジャスティンは実験室で化学の担当教員である沖教授と実験の話をしています。会話では、注意したり、確認したりする際の表現を学びます。また、文法では<u>不定詞</u>、読解では<u>単位3（温度）</u>に焦点を当てて学習します。

 ## Warm-up

授業前に確認しておこう！

Vocabulary Preview

🎧 1-50

1～10 の語句の意味として適切なものを a～j の中から選びましょう。

1. equipment	_____	a. 有毒な	
2. liquid	_____	b. 液体、液体の	
3. give off	_____	c. 蒸気	
4. vapor	_____	d. （程度などが）非常に	
5. melt	_____	e. （液体を通す）管、筒	
6. crystal	_____	f. 結晶	
7. toxic	_____	g. 機器、機材	
8. highly	_____	h. （温度の単位の）度	
9. degree	_____	i. （気体・熱など）を発する	
10. tube	_____	j. 溶ける	

ビートに乗って 1～10 の語句を発音してみましょう。

Grammar Point : 不定詞

It's a good idea **to check** the data again. （データを再度確認することは良い考えです）

I'm ready **to start** the experiment. （私は実験を始める準備ができています）

I need someone **to help** me with this experiment.

（この実験で私を手伝ってくれる人が必要です）

≪ to ＋動詞の原形≫の形を <u>to 不定詞</u>または単に<u>不定詞</u>と呼びますが、その用法は下の表のように大きく 3 つに分けられます。

名詞的用法	～すること	I want **to welcome** you to our project.
副詞的用法	～するために（目的）	I stayed up late **to prepare** for the final exam.
	～して（感情の原因）	We're very happy **to have** you in our team.
形容詞的用法	～すべき	I have a favor **to ask** you.

形容詞的用法は名詞のすぐ後ろにきてその名詞を説明します。「頼むべきお願いを持っている」→「お願いがある」

また、下の表のように、to 不定詞の前に what や how などの疑問詞がついてまとまった意味を表す他、《形容詞／副詞 +enough+to 不定詞》といった慣用表現もあります。例文の日本語訳を完成させながら使い方を確認しましょう。

疑問詞 +to 不定詞	《 how+to 不定詞》で「どのように〜したらよいのか、〜の仕方」となります。 Let me show you <u>how to use</u> this equipment. （　　　　　　　　　　　　　　　）
動詞 + 人 +to 不定詞	《 want+ 人 +to 不定詞》で「〜に…してほしい」となります。 What do you <u>want me to do</u>? （　　　　　　　　　　　　　　）
enough や too を伴う 形容詞／副詞 +to 不定詞	《形容詞／副詞 +enough+to 不定詞》で「〜するには十分なくらい…だ」となります。 Sarah was <u>kind enough to check</u> the data of the experiment. （　　　　　　　　　　　　） 《 too+ 形容詞／副詞 +to 不定詞》で「〜するにはあまりにも…すぎる」となります。 I was <u>too tired to check</u> the data of the experiment by myself. （　　　　　　　　　　　　）

 ## Let's Listen!

会話の大意を聞き取ろう！

ジャスティンと沖教授の会話を聞いて、質問に対する答えとして最も適切なものを(A) 〜 (C) の中から１つ選びましょう。 1-51

Question 1 What does the professor ask Justin to do?

(A) Prepare the equipment
(B) Explain what he's going to do
(C) Set up the test tube

Question 2 What is true of the vapor?

(A) It has no color.
(B) It gives off a nice smell.
(C) It's toxic.

Question 3 According to Justin, what is important?

(A) To see the liquid stage
(B) To clean the test tube
(C) To collect all the vapor

1. スクリプトを見ながら会話をもう1度聞き、下線部に当てはまる表現を書き入れましょう。（下線部には単語が2つ入ります） 1-51

2. 内容を確認して、全文を音読してみましょう。

3. ジャスティンと沖教授とお客の役割をパートナーと一緒に演じてみましょう。

Let's Practice the Roleplay!

Justin's Role   Professor's Role

Justin and Professor Oki are talking in the laboratory.

Justin: I think the equipment is all ready now.

Professor: That looks good. I think you're ready ①＿＿＿＿＿＿＿＿ your experiment. Can you explain ②＿＿＿＿＿＿＿＿ going to do?

Justin: So, I've put the iodine[1] crystals in the ③＿＿＿＿＿＿＿＿ , and next I'm going to heat it.

Professor: Good! But be careful ④＿＿＿＿＿＿＿＿ overheat it.

Justin: Right. And at first, it'll give off a purple vapor. ⑤＿＿＿＿＿＿＿＿ if it overheats?

Professor: Well, you'll probably miss the ⑥＿＿＿＿＿＿＿＿ . Also, remember that the vapor is highly toxic.

Justin: OK, I'll be really careful. It's important to be ⑦＿＿＿＿＿＿＿＿ see the liquid stage before it turns to vapor, right?

Professor: That's right. It should reach its ⑧＿＿＿＿＿＿＿＿ at around 114 degrees Celsius[2].

[Notes] 1. ヨウ素（常温では固体だが、加熱すると気体へ変化する。融点は 113.6 ℃）2. 摂氏（温度の単位）

 **音読のヒント**

単語の最後にくる l [l] の発音は Unit 7 で取り上げましたが、会話に出てくる crystal や purple の最後にくる [l] もやはり「ル」ではなく「ゥ」のように聞こえます。「クリスタル」や「パープル」のようなカタカナ英語の発音にならないように注意しましょう。実際の発音はそれぞれ「クリストゥ」、「パーポゥ」といった感じです。

Grammar

A. 例にならい、枠の中から適切な単語を選び、必要な場合は適切な形にして次の 1 〜 4 の文を完成させましょう。

例 Would you like something (*to drink*) ?

prepare
drink ✓
sign
hand
bother

1. I'm sorry (　　　　　) you, but could you help me?

2. Is it OK (　　　　　) in the homework tomorrow?

3. I'd like (　　　　　) up for a course in information ethics.

4. Sarah stayed up late in order (　　　　　) for her presentation.

B. 例にならい、カッコ内から正しい語句を選び○で囲みましょう。

例 I want (join (to join)) your research project.

1. Let me (show / to show) you how this machine works.

2. I have a favor (ask / to ask) you.

3. Rob was (kind enough / enough kind) to explain the project in detail.

4. I'd like (some / to some) information on this program.

C. 日本語の意味に合うようにカッコ内の語句を並べ替え、英文を完成させましょう。ただし、文の始めにくる単語も小文字にしてあり、1 つ余分な語句が含まれています。

1 喜んであなたのプロジェクトをお手伝いします。
(to / I'm / your / happy / helping / help) project.

_____

2. 私に何をしてほしいのですか？
(do you / me / to do / want / want to / what)?

_____

3. その機器の使い方を教えてあげましょう。
I'll show you (the / how / what / to / use / equipment).

_____

4. サラにデータの確認を頼みましょう。
(the data / Sarah / check / ask / let's / to check).

_____

Let's Read!

次のパッセージを読み、その内容について 1〜3 の質問に答えましょう。

 1-52

Is That in Fahrenheit or Celsius?

Visitors to the U.S. may notice a cultural difference as soon as they leave the airport. On a hot summer day, you might be shocked to see the temperature outside the car may be over 95°. But don't worry. That's Fahrenheit, not Celsius! It's just 35°C. Fahrenheit and Celsius are both scales used to measure temperature based on the freezing and boiling points of water. The freezing point of water in Celsius is zero degrees and the boiling point is 100 degrees, [＿＿＿] in Fahrenheit, water freezes at 32 degrees and boils at 212 degrees. Globally, Celsius is the standard. Only a small number of countries and territories, including the United States, still use Fahrenheit.

1. The freezing and boiling points of water _____ for both Fahrenheit and Celsius.

   (A) cannot be measured

   (B) provide the basis

   (C) are basically the same

2. The word that belongs in the [＿＿＿] in this passage is _____ .

   (A) because

   (B) while

   (C) so

3. Which sentence is true?

   (A) Visitors to the U.S. may be shocked by the heat when they leave the airport.

   (B) The U.S. is the only country that uses the Fahrenheit scale.

   (C) Water boils at 212 degrees Fahrenheit.

Notes

temperature: 温度　95°: = 95 degrees　Fahrenheit: 華氏　Celsius: 摂氏

＊摂氏と華氏の関係は次の式のようになる。　摂氏（℃）=｛華氏（℉）−32｝÷1.8

Challenge Yourself!

Part I Photographs

（A）〜（C）の英文を聞き、写真の描写として最も適切なものを選びましょう。 1-53

1.

（A）　　　（B）　　　（C）

2.

（A）　　　（B）　　　（C）

Part II Question-Response

最初に聞こえてくる英文に対する応答として最も適切なものを（A）〜（C）の中から選びましょう。 1-54

3.　（A）　　　（B）　　　（C）

4.　（A）　　　（B）　　　（C）

Part III Short Conversations

会話を聞き、下の英文が会話の内容と合っていれば T（True）、間違っていれば F（False）を○で囲みましょう。 1-55

5. The man wants the woman to explain how to do the experiment.　　　T　　　F

6. The test tubes in the cupboard are too big.　　　T　　　F

 Let's Read Aloud & Write!

授業のまとめとして、今日学習した対話文を3回書き写してしっかり覚えましょう。1度英文を声に出して読んでから書き写すと頭に残りやすくなります。

┤ **今日のまとめ** ├

英語で答えられますか？　　　Which do you like better, experiments or lectures?

Unit 10
I totally forgot to write my report.

文法 ▶ 形容詞・副詞

ミナコは学生ラウンジで久しぶりにジャスティンを見かけ、彼に話しかけます。会話では、近況を尋ねたり、理解を示したりする際の表現を学びます。また、文法では形容詞・副詞、読解では人体2（血液）に焦点を当てて学習します。

 Warm-up　　　　　　　　　　授業前に確認しておこう！

Vocabulary Preview　　　　　　　　　　🎧 1-56

1〜10 の語句の意味として適切なものを a〜j の中から選びましょう。

1. totally	_____	a. 〜を取り除く
2. in a while	_____	b. 〜を送る
3. intercultural	_____	c. 固体
4. mean	_____	d. 期限が来て
5. essential	_____	e. 〜を意味する
6. deliver	_____	f. 異文化間の
7. remove	_____	g. 感染症
8. infection	_____	h. 完全に、まったく
9. due	_____	i. しばらくの間
10. solid	_____	j. 不可欠な

ビートに乗って 1〜10 の語句を発音してみましょう。

Grammar Point : 形容詞・副詞

It's an <u>interesting</u> experiment. You'll enjoy it.

　　　　　　　　（それは興味深い実験です。楽しいですよ）［形容詞］

I <u>almost</u> missed the experiment.

　　　　　　　　（私はもう少しで実験に参加できなくなるところでした）［副詞］

　　<u>形容詞</u>は、1 番目の例文における interesting のように、<u>名詞と結びついて人やものの状態や性質を説明するもの</u>です。形容詞は名詞の直前に置かれる他、"The experiment is interesting." のように、動詞の後に置いて主語（＝名詞・代名詞）に説明を加えたりします。それに対し、<u>副詞</u>は、2 番目の例文における almost のように、動詞や形容詞、他の副詞といった<u>名詞以外のものと結びついて様子や場所、時、頻度などを説明するもの</u>です。次の表で副詞の種類を確認しましょう。

「様態」（どのように）を表す	well, fast など	Could you speak more **slowly**? I can't follow you.
「場所」（どこで）を表す	here, home など	I'll go **home** after I finish this experiment.
「時」（いつ）を表す	late, soon など	I came home very **late** at night.
「頻度」（どれくらいの度合いで）を表す	always, often など	一般動詞の前、be 動詞・助動詞の後に置くのが基本です。 Justin **always** carries his laptop. I can **never** be bored with science.
「程度」（どれだけ）を表す	barely, hardly など	I'm sorry I can't help you. I **hardly** know where to start.

修飾する語句の直前が基本。ただし動詞を修飾する場合は一般動詞の前、be 動詞・助動詞の後に置きます。

　一般に、副詞は usually や easily のように -ly で終わるものが多いですが、hard（懸命に、激しく）と hardly（ほとんど〜でない）、late（遅れて）と lately（最近）のように、似た副詞で意味の異なるものがあります。また、形容詞に関しても、few と a few や little と a little など、a の有無で意味が異なりますので注意が必要です。

　下の例文の日本語訳を完成させながら使い方を確認しましょう。

a few は「（数について）少しはある」、few は「（数について）ほとんどない」となります。

Don't worry. We have **a few** more days before the deadline.
(   )

a little は「（量について）少しはある」、little は「（量について）ほとんどない」となります。

I have **little** experience in animal experiments.
(   )

 Let's Listen!　　　　　　　　　　　会話の大意を聞き取ろう！

ミナコとジャスティンの会話を聞いて、質問に対する答えとして最も適切なものを
(A) ～（C）の中から１つ選びましょう。　　　 1-57

Question 1　　When is the deadline for Justin's report?

(A) Today
(B) Tomorrow
(C) The day after tomorrow

Question 2　　What is his report about?

(A) Intercultural communication
(B) Intercultural education
(C) International communication

Question 3　　Is he writing his report in Japanese?

(A) Yes, he has no trouble in writing Japanese.
(B) Yes, but he's having a lot of difficulty.
(C) No, he isn't.

Let's Check & Read Aloud!

1. スクリプトを見ながら会話をもう１度聞き、下線部に当てはまる表現を書き入 1-57
   れましょう。（下線部には単語が２つ入ります）
2. 内容を確認して、全文を音読してみましょう。
3. ミナコとジャスティンの役割をパートナーと一緒に演じてみ
   ましょう。

Let's Practice the Roleplay!

Minako's Role   Justin's Role

Minako speaks to Justin at the student lounge.

Minako Hi, Justin. I ①_____ you in a while! How are you doing?

Justin Hi, Minako. Actually, not so good. I ②_____ to write my report
and ③_____ tomorrow!

Minako Don't worry. You'll be fine. What are you writing about?

Justin Intercultural communication. I'm writing about ④_____ I had
when I came here last year. I didn't understand much Japanese at that time.

Minako Then, you have a lot ⑤_____ about.

Justin I certainly do.

Minako By the way, are you writing it in Japanese?

Justin No way! I can understand Japanese, but writing Japanese is ⑥_____
_____ for me.

Minako I see ⑦_____ mean. Well, I've got to go. ⑧_____
with your report.

Justin Thanks. I'm going to need it!

 聞き取りのヒント

"Well, I've got to go." の have got to は have to（〜しないといけない）と同じ意味でよく使われ
ますが、got to の部分は「ガット・トゥ」と発音されると思っていると聞き取れないかもしれませ
ん。Unit 3 で取り上げたように、同じ子音が連続する場合、同じ音が繰り返されるのではなく、前の
子音が発音されず、その音が聞こえなくなり、「ガットゥ」のように聞こえます。また、実際の会話
では got to は gotta [gáṭə, gɔ́ṭə]「ガタ、ガラ、ゴタ」のように発音され、さらに have も省略して "I
gotta go." と発音されることもよくあります。

 **Grammar**

A. 例にならい、枠の中から適切な単語を選んで次の 1 ～ 4 の文を完成させましょう。

例　Minako speaks English very (well).

1. It is said that (　　　　　) much sun causes skin cancer.

2. I wasn't prepared for the exam. I (　　　　) passed it.

3. Dr. Johnson has (　　　　　) experience in teaching.

4. How (　　　　　) can you finish the assignment?

> barely
> little
> soon
> too
> well ✓

B. 例にならい、カッコ内から正しい語句を選び○で囲みましょう。

例　How long does it take to go (there / to there)?

1. This experiment won't take (much / many) time.

2. You have to be very (careful / carefully) when you conduct an experiment.

3. Minako is really (good / well) at mathematics.

4. It will take (a few / a little) days to analyze the data.

C. 日本語の意味に合うようにカッコ内の語句を並べ替え、英文を完成させましょう。ただし、文の始めにくる単語も小文字にしてあり、1 つ余分な語句が含まれています。

1. レポートの締め切りまでに数時間あります。
   (a few / few / before / we / hours / the / have) deadline for the report.

   _____

2. 私のレポートは短すぎるかもしれません。
   (short / my report / be / enough / too / might).

   _____

3. 期末試験の勉強で忙しいです。
   I'm busy (studying / exams / finally / final / for / the).

   _____

4. 私は動物実験をしたことがありません。
   I've (animals / done / on / ever / never / experiments).

   _____

次のパッセージを読み、その内容について 1〜3 の質問に答えましょう。 1-58

Blood

Blood is essential to life. It delivers oxygen and nutrients around your body so it can keep working. It also carries carbon dioxide and other waste materials to the lungs, kidneys, and digestive system, to be removed from the body. [   ], it fights infections, and carries hormones around the body.

Over half your blood is plasma, salts, and protein. The rest of your blood contains solids—red and white blood cells, and platelets. Red blood cells deliver oxygen from your lungs to your tissues and organs. White blood cells fight infections. Platelets help blood to clot when you have a cut.

---

1. The word or phrase that belongs in the [   ] in this passage is _____ .

   (A) However

   (B) In addition

   (C) For example

2. The primary function of white blood cells is to _____ .

   (A) protect us against disease

   (B) defend us against waste materials

   (C) deliver oxygen from the heart to the lungs

3. Which sentence is true?

   (A) Red and white blood cells make up more than 50% of our body's blood.

   (B) Carbon dioxide is required to maintain bodily functions.

   (C) Platelets help to stop bleeding when you have a cut.

Components of Blood

PLASMA
about 55%

WHITE BLOOD CELLS
about 4%

RED BLOOD CELLS
about 41%

Notes

nutrient: 栄養素　digestive system：消化器官　plasma: 血しょう（血液で、血球を除いた液体成分）　platelet: 血小板　tissue: 組織　clot：凝固する

Challenge Yourself!

Part I **Photographs**

（A）～（C）の英文を聞き、写真の描写として最も適切なものを選びましょう。 1-59

1.

(A)　　　(B)　　　(C)

2.

(A)　　　(B)　　　(C)

Part II **Question-Response**

最初に聞こえてくる英文に対する応答として最も適切なものを（A）～（C）の中 1-60
から選びましょう。

3.　(A)　　　(B)　　　(C)

4.　(A)　　　(B)　　　(C)

Part III **Short Conversations**

会話を聞き、下の英文が会話の内容と合っていれば T（True）、間違っていれば 1-61
F（False）を○で囲みましょう。

5. The man prefers reading Japanese to speaking it.　　　　　T　　　　F

6. The woman thinks the man has made a mistake with the date.　　　T　　　　F

 Let's Read Aloud & Write!

授業のまとめとして、今日学習した対話文を３回書き写して
しっかり覚えましょう。１度英文を声に出して読んでから書き
写すと頭に残りやすくなります。

┤ **今日のまとめ** ├

英語で答えられますか？　　　Do you always submit your homework before the deadline?

Unit 11 This is still a beta version.

ミナコとロブは学生食堂でアプリ開発について話をしています。会話では、興味を示したり、例示したりする際の表現を学びます。また、文法では**分詞**、読解では**ロボット**に焦点を当てて学習します。

Warm-up

授業前に確認しておこう！

Vocabulary Preview

🎵 1-62

1～10 の語句の意味として適切なものを a～j の中から選びましょう。

1. app	＿＿＿＿	a. 自分自身の
2. option	＿＿＿＿	b. ～を許す、許可する
3. impression	＿＿＿＿	c. 選択肢、選択できるもの
4. record	＿＿＿＿	d. 衛星、衛星を利用した
5. allow	＿＿＿＿	e. 化身
6. try out	＿＿＿＿	f. 印象
7. own	＿＿＿＿	g. 開発する
8. develop	＿＿＿＿	h. 試しに使う
9. satellite	＿＿＿＿	i. アプリ（application program の省略形）
10. avatar	＿＿＿＿	j. ～を録画する、～を記録する

ビートに乗って 1～10 の語句を発音してみましょう。

Grammar Point : 分詞

Who is the girl giving the presentation with Justin?
（ジャスティンと一緒にプレゼンをしている女性は誰ですか？）［現在分詞］

Books borrowed from the library need to be returned within two weeks.
（図書館で借りられた本は 2 週間以内に返却される必要があります）［過去分詞］

　分詞には**現在分詞**と**過去分詞**があり、これらは形容詞として使うことができます。上の例文のように、**現在分詞は「～している」という能動的な意味、過去分詞は「～された」という受動的な意味になります。**

　形容詞には分詞から派生しているものがあり、感情を表す動詞から派生しているものは使い分けに注意が必要です。例えば、exciting と excited はもともと動詞 excite（「（人）を興奮させる」）のそれぞれ現在分詞、過去分詞なので、exciting は「（人を）興奮させるような」という能動の意味、excited は「興奮させられた（⇒興奮した）」という受動の意味を持ちます。次の表でそうした形容詞の使い方を確認しましょう。

-ing （物や事がどのようなものかを説明する）	-ed （人がどのように感じたかを説明する）
This experiment is ⌈ boring. （退屈な） exciting. （刺激的な） └ interesting. （面白い）	I'm ⌈ bored. （退屈している） excited. （興奮している） └ interested. （興味を持っている）

例文の日本語訳を完成させながら分詞の用法を確認しましょう。

> 1 語の場合は名詞の前に置きます。

We need to restore the <u>lost</u> data somehow.

(   )

> 他の語句が加わると名詞の後に置きます。

A handout is a document <u>given to students in class</u>.

(   )

> 「have + 目的語 + 過去分詞」で「〜を…してもらう、…される」となります。

<u>I had my English homework **checked**</u> by Justin.

(   )

> 「keep + 目的語 + 補語」で「〜をずっと（…の状態に）しておく」となります。

Don't <u>leave your homework **unfinished**</u>.

 ## Let's Listen!

会話の大意を聞き取ろう！

 1-63

ミナコとロブの会話を聞いて、質問に対する答えとして最も適切なものを（A）〜（C）
の中から 1 つ選びましょう。

Question 1　What are they talking about?

(A) An app Rob bought recently
(B) An app Rob has been developing
(C) An app Rob's friend has been developing

Question 2　What is true of the app?

(A) You can create a video with it.
(B) It doesn't use satellite technology.
(C) It has a voice changing option.

Question 3　Has Rob found any problems with it?

(A) Yes, it sometimes freezes.
(B) No, he thinks it's perfect.
(C) No, but he's going to add an option.

Let's Check & Read Aloud!

1. スクリプトを見ながら会話をもう1度聞き、下線部に当てはまる表現を書き入れましょう。（下線部には単語が2つ入ります） 1-63
2. 内容を確認して、全文を音読してみましょう。
3. ミナコとロブの役割をパートナーと一緒に演じてみましょう。

Let's Practice the Roleplay!

Minako's Role   Rob's Role

Minako is chatting with Rob in the school cafeteria.

Minako	That looks interesting.
Rob	Yeah, it's a prototype[1] of a ①_____ that I've been developing.
Minako	Does it use ②_____ to track your trips?
Rob	Yeah, but this one ③_____ to create a video with your own avatar.
Minako	That's cool! So, for example, if I visit Rome, I can record the trip as a 3D me[2], right?
Rob	Yeah, you can record your impressions and ④_____ , too.
Minako	It looks like a ⑤_____ fun.
Rob	It sure is. But this is still a beta version[3].
Minako	Have you found ⑥_____ with it?
Rob	Not really, but I'm going ⑦_____ a voice changing option.
Minako	That's a good idea. Not many people like hearing their own voices when ⑧_____ !

[NOTES]
1. 試作品　2.3次元の私　3.ベータ版（開発中のソフトウェアなどのうち、完成間近の段階にあるもの）

 音読のヒント

会話の中で使われていた a lot of は、「ア・ロット・オブ」ではなく、「アロッロブ」のように聞こえます。音がつながるだけなら「アロットブ」になりそうですが、アメリカ英語では [t] が母音に挟まれた場合、ラ行に近い音になります。

Grammar

文法に強くなろう！

A. 例にならい、枠の中から適切な単語を選び、現在分詞か過去分詞にして次の 1 〜 4 の文を完成させましょう。

例　The language (*spoken*) in Brazil is Portuguese.

1. It took a few hours to restore the (　　　　　) data.

2. The gate remained (　　　　　), so I couldn't enter the laboratory.

3. I'm very sorry to keep you (　　　　　).

4. Did you have trouble (　　　　　) the questions?

close
answer
wait
speak ✓
lose

B. 例にならい、カッコ内から正しい語句を選び○で囲みましょう。

例　Chemistry is very (interesting / interested).

1. We're (exciting / excited) to work with Dr. Miller.

2. You shouldn't leave your project (unfinishing / unfinished).

3. We have only two days (leaving / left) before the presentation.

4. A beaker is a glass container (using / used) in chemistry.

C. 日本語の意味に合うようにカッコ内の語句を並べ替え、英文を完成させましょう。ただし、文の始めにくる単語も小文字にしてあり、1 つ余分な語句が含まれています。

1. 私はそのアプリの開発で忙しいです。
(developing / I'm / app / busy / the / developed).

_____

2. ロブにノートパソコンを修理してもらいました。
I had (fixed / fixing / laptop / Rob / by / my).

_____

3. そのアプリはとても退屈だと感じました。
(bored / boring / found / the app / very / I).

_____

4. 実験用白衣を着ている男性がスミス博士です。
The man (Dr. Smith / is / worn / wearing / lab coat / a).

_____

71

次のパッセージを読み、その内容について 1～3 の質問に答えましょう。 1-64

Where Did Robots Come From?

The word "robot" entered the English language after appearing in Czech writer Karel Čapek's science-fiction play *R.U.R.* in 1920. Taking their name from the Eastern European word, *robota*, meaning "forced labor" or "hard work," robots were machines created to serve humans. The robots' role as servants to humans soon captured the public imagination. Recent developments in robotics and Artificial Intelligence (A.I.) worry some people, perhaps with good reason. ⬚, the robots in Čapek's play served their human masters, but later revolted, causing the <u>extinction</u> of the human race. Maybe we shouldn't be asking "Where did robots come from?" Instead, we should ask "Where are robots going to?"

---

1. What is the main message of the passage?

   (A) The history of robotics began in the Czech Republic in the early 20th century.

   (B) The role of robots is to serve humans.

   (C) We should be careful about how we make progress with technology.

2. The phrase that belongs in the ⬚ in this passage is _____ .

   (A) In addition

   (B) At first

   (C) As a result

3. The underlined word "extinction" means that _____ .

   (A) all members of a species die

   (B) members of a group become very rich

   (C) some members of a species become controlled by others

Scene from *R.U.R.* (*Rossum's Universal Robots*) as a TV play.

 Notes

Czech: チェコ人の、チェコ語の   Karel Čapek: カレル・チャペック

servant: 召使い   robotics: ロボット工学

Challenge Yourself!

Part I   Photographs

（A）〜（C）の英文を聞き、写真の描写として最も適切なものを選びましょう。   1-65

1.

(A)   (B)   (C)

2.

(A)   (B)   (C)

Part II   Question-Response

最初に聞こえてくる英文に対する応答として最も適切なものを（A）〜（C）の中から選びましょう。   1-66

3.   (A)   (B)   (C)

4.   (A)   (B)   (C)

Part III   Short Conversations

会話を聞き、下の英文が会話の内容と合っていれば T（True）、間違っていれば F（False）を○で囲みましょう。 1-67

5. The man created the app.   T   F

6. The man is a regular listener to gaming podcasts.   T   F

 # Let's Read Aloud & Write!

授業のまとめとして、今日学習した対話文を3回書き写してしっかり覚えましょう。1度英文を声に出して読んでから書き写すと頭に残りやすくなります。

┤ 今日のまとめ ├

英語で答えられますか？　　　Are you interested in developing new apps?

Unit 12 I'm thinking of joining the course.

ミナコは学生食堂でロブに話しかけます。相談したいことがあるようです。会話では、意見を尋ねたり、励ましたりする際の表現を学びます。また、文法では**動名詞**、読解では**元素 1（元素周期表）**に焦点を当てて学習します。

 ## Warm-up

授業前に確認しておこう！

Vocabulary Preview

CD 2-01

1～10 の語句の意味として適切なものを a ～ j の中から選びましょう。

1. regret	＿＿＿＿	a. 緊張して
2. chemistry	＿＿＿＿	b. 工業の、技術の、専門的な
3. abroad	＿＿＿＿	c. 後悔する
4. nervous	＿＿＿＿	d. 傑作、名作
5. originally	＿＿＿＿	e. 海外に、外国へ
6. masterpiece	＿＿＿＿	f. パンフレット
7. organize	＿＿＿＿	g. 体系づける、まとめる
8. definitely	＿＿＿＿	h. もともと、最初は
9. technical	＿＿＿＿	i. 絶対に、もちろん
10. brochure	＿＿＿＿	j. 化学

ビートに乗って 1～10 の語句を発音してみましょう。

Grammar Point : 動名詞

<u>Seeing</u> is <u>believing</u>.　（見ることは信じること⇒百聞は一見に如かず）［主語や補語になる］

I really enjoyed <u>doing</u> a lot of experiments with you.

　　（あなたといろんな実験をすることができて本当に楽しかったです）［動詞の目的語になる］

I'm thinking of <u>joining</u> the fieldwork.

　　　　　　　（フィールドワークに参加することを考えています）［前置詞の目的語になる］

　動詞の ing 形は現在分詞として「～している」という意味で使われますが、それとは別に「～すること」のように動詞を名詞化する場合にも使われ、これを**動名詞**と言います。動詞が名詞の働きをするものには to 不定詞もありますが、3 番目の例文のように前置詞の後には to 不定詞ではなく必ず動名詞を使います。この他にも動名詞と to 不定詞には注意すべき用法がありますので、次の表で確認しましょう。

必ず動名詞を目的語とする動詞	enjoy, finish, mind, stop, suggest, etc.
必ず to 不定詞を目的語とする動詞	expect, hope, learn, mean, want, etc.
どちらも目的語とする動詞	begin, like, love, start, etc.
動名詞か to 不定詞かで意味が異なる動詞	forget, remember, try, etc. 動名詞は「すでに起きたこと」、to 不定詞は「これから先のこと」と覚えておくとよいでしょう。 ex.) I'll never **forget visiting** this laboratory. （～したことを忘れる） ex.) I totally **forgot to submit** the report. （～し忘れる）

また、下の表に挙げる表現では動名詞がよく使われます。

be used to ...	～に慣れている
feel like ...	～したい気がする
How about ...?	～してはどうですか
Would you mind ...?	～していただけませんか

下の例文の日本語訳を完成させながら使い方を確認しましょう。

How about joining our research group?
( )

Sorry. I'm not used to working in a group.
( )

 Let's Listen!　　　　　　　会話の大意を聞き取ろう！

ミナコとロブの会話を聞いて、質問に対する答えとして最も適切なものを(A)～(C) 2-02
の中から１つ選びましょう。

Question 1　Has Minako ever been abroad?

(A) Yes, but only once.
(B) Yes, a few times.
(C) No, she hasn't.

Question 2　How did Rob feel before coming to Japan?

(A)　Excited
(B)　Happy
(C)　Worried

Question 3　What does he suggest at the end of the conversation?

(A)　She should join the program.
(B)　She should think twice about the program.
(C)　She should study abroad for a year.

Let's Check & Read Aloud!

音読してみよう！

1. スクリプトを見ながら会話をもう１度聞き、下線部に当てはまる表現を書き入れましょう。（下線部には単語が２つ入ります） 2-02

2. 内容を確認して、全文を音読してみましょう。

3. ミナコとロブの役割をパートナーと一緒に演じてみましょう。

Let's Practice the Roleplay!

Minako's Role　　Rob's Role

Minako speaks to Rob at the school cafeteria.

| Minako | Rob, can I talk to you for a minute? I ①_____ advice. |

| Rob | Sure. How can I ②_____ ? |

| Minako | Look at this brochure. It's for a summer English course for science majors. What do you think? |

| Rob | Well, it's a great program. You can learn technical English. Also, you can learn a lot about American culture. |

| Minako | Yes, I'm thinking ③_____ the course, but I'm a little nervous. I've never ④_____ . |

| Rob | Don't worry. Most people would feel the same way. In fact, I was very nervous ⑤_____ to Japan. |

| Minako | Oh, really? |

| Rob | But I've ⑥_____ a great time here since then. I'm sure this program would be a great experience for you. |

| Minako | ⑦_____ try it? |

| Rob | Definitely. You won't ⑧_____ . |

 **音読のヒント**

Unit 1 で同化について触れましたが、did のように、[d] で終わる単語のすぐ後に [j] で始まる単語が来た場合、２つの音が一緒になって [dʒ]「ヂュ」という別の音に変わります。Did you や Could you などの例がよく知られていますが、会話の中に出てきた need your もその一例で、「ニード・ユア」ではなく、「ニージョア」のように発音されます。音読する際に気をつけましょう。

Grammar

A. 例にならい、枠の中から適切な単語を選び、動名詞か to 不定詞にして次の 1 ～ 4 の文を完成させましょう。

> 例　Thank you for (*answering*) my question.

| listen |
| become |
| speak |
| make |
| answer ✓ |

1. I'm not good at (　　　　　) in front of people.

2. I hope (　　　　　) a scientist.

3. Don't be afraid of (　　　　　) mistakes in class.

4. We enjoy (　　　　　) to classical music.

B. 例にならい、カッコ内から正しい語句を選び○で囲みましょう。

> 例　Sarah wants (to join / joining) the fieldwork.

1. I expect (finishing / to finish) the report by tomorrow.

2. We look forward to (work / working) with you again.

3. Minako needs to practice (speaking / to speak) English more.

4. How about (making / to make) a homepage for our club?

C. 日本語の意味に合うようにカッコ内の語句を並べ替え、英文を完成させましょう。ただし、文の始めにくる単語も小文字にしてあり、1 つ余分な語句が含まれています。

1. 今夜は外食したい気分です。

(eating / feel / to eat / I / out / like) tonight.

_____

2. 英語を話すことに慣れています。

(English / to / speaking / I'm / speak / used).

_____

3. 忘れずにレポートを提出してください。

(submit / submitting / don't / to / your report / forget).

_____

4. これを手伝ってもらえませんか？

(helping / mind / would / to help / me / you) with this?

_____

 **Let's Read!**

次のパッセージを読み、その内容について 1〜3 の質問に答えましょう。 2-03

The Periodic Table of Elements

The periodic table of elements is a masterpiece of scientific design. Originally created by Russian scientist, Dmitri Mendeleev, it organizes elements according to two standards: by <u>common properties</u>, and by atomic weight. The modern table is, ⬚ , organized by atomic number. The elements are named in various ways. Some, such as Einsteinium, are named after famous people. Thorium is named after Thor, the Scandinavian god of thunder. Uranium was named after the discovery of the planet Uranus. Others, such as Nihonium, and Moscovium, are named after the places where they were discovered. Polonium was named after the country of Marie Curie's birth—Poland.

---

1. The underlined phrase "common properties" means _____ .

   (A) shared characteristics

   (B) atomic numbers

   (C) different elements

2. The word or phrase that belongs in the ⬚ in this passage is _____ .

   (A) for example

   (B) therefore

   (C) however

3. Which sentence is true?

   (A) Nihonium and Moscovium are named after countries.

   (B) The names of elements are given in a variety of ways.

   (C) Elements are often named after their discoverer.

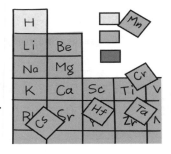

📖 **Notes**

Dmitri Mendeleev: ドミトリ・メンデレーエフ	Einsteinium: アインスタイニウム（原子番号 99 の元素）
Thorium: トリウム（原子番号 90 の元素）	Thor: トール
Uranium: ウラン（原子番号 92 の元素）	Nihonium: ニホニウム（原子番号 113 の元素）
Moscovium: モスコビウム（原子番号 115 の元素）	Polonium: ポロニウム（原子番号 84 の元素）

Challenge Yourself!

Part I Photographs

(A)〜(C) の英文を聞き、写真の描写として最も適切なものを選びましょう。   2-04

1.

    (A)   (B)   (C)

2.

    (A)   (B)   (C)

Part II Question-Response

最初に聞こえてくる英文に対する応答として最も適切なものを（A）〜（C）の中から選びましょう。   2-05

3. (A)   (B)   (C)

4. (A)   (B)   (C)

Part III Short Conversations

会話を聞き、下の英文が会話の内容と合っていれば T（True）、間違っていれば F（False）を○で囲みましょう。   2-06

5. The woman decides not to study biochemistry.   T   F

6. The man used to be the woman's student.   T   F

 Let's Read Aloud & Write!

音読筆写で覚えよう！

授業のまとめとして、今日学習した対話文を 3 回書き写してしっかり覚えましょう。1 度英文を声に出して読んでから書き写すと頭に残りやすくなります。

┤ **今日のまとめ** ├

英語で答えられますか？   Do you want to take a summer English course?

Unit 13 I have to study for the exams.

文法 ▶ 関係詞

期末試験前のある日、ジャスティンとミナコは学生ラウンジで話をしています。会話では、説明したり、提案したりする際の表現を学びます。また、文法では関係詞、読解では元素 2（水素）に焦点を当てて学習します。

Warm-up

授業前に確認しておこう！

Vocabulary Preview

 2-07

1〜10 の語句の意味として適切なものを a 〜 j の中から選びましょう。

1. basic	＿＿＿＿	a. その上、さらに
2. substance	＿＿＿＿	b. 休む、くつろぐ
3. trust	＿＿＿＿	c. 胃、おなか
4. react	＿＿＿＿	d. 基礎の、基本的な
5. positive	＿＿＿＿	e. 減らす
6. reduce	＿＿＿＿	f. 反応する
7. besides	＿＿＿＿	g. 実行する、行う
8. stomach	＿＿＿＿	h. 確信して
9. take it easy	＿＿＿＿	i. 〜を信用する
10. carry out	＿＿＿＿	j. 物質

ビートに乗って 1〜10 の語句を発音してみましょう。

Grammar Point : 関係詞

We need <u>someone</u> **who** can help with this experiment.

（私たちにはこの実験を手伝ってくれる人が必要です）

I have <u>a friend</u> **whose** father is a famous chemist.

（私には父親が有名な化学者である友人がいます）

We enjoyed watching <u>the video</u> **that** Justin made.

（私たちはジャスティンが作ったビデオを楽しんで見ました）

　「この実験を手伝ってくれる人」のように、下線部分と名詞（この場合は「人」）をつなぐ（関係づける）働きをするのが関係代名詞です。**関係代名詞**で説明される名詞を**先行詞**と呼びますが、その先行詞が人かそうでないかによって関係代名詞は次の表のような使い分けをします。

先行詞	主格	所有格	目的格
人	who	whose	who/whom
人以外	which	whose	which
人・人以外	that	—	that

> 目的格の関係代名詞はよく省略されます。また、口語ではthat 以外はあまり使われません。

1番目の例文は次の2つの文を1つにしたものと考えればよいでしょう。

A. We need <u>someone</u>.
B. <u>He</u> can help with this experiment.

➡ We need someone **who** can help with this experiment.

下線部分の someone と he は同一人物なのでここを関係代名詞でつなぐわけですが、he は元の文の主語なので主格の関係代名詞 who を使います。同様に、3番目の例文は次の2文を1つにしたものです。下線部分の a video と it が同一のものなのでここを関係代名詞でつなぎ、it は元の文の目的語なので目的格の関係代名詞 that を使います。

A. Justin made <u>a video</u>.
B. We enjoyed watching <u>it</u>.

➡ We enjoyed watching the video **that** Justin made.

下の例文の日本語訳を完成させながら使い方を確認しましょう。

Please let me know if there is anything else I can help with.

(　　　　　　　　　　　　　)

Feel free to tell me <u>whatever</u> you need.

(　　　　　　　　　　　　　)

> 関係代名詞には先行詞を含むものがあり、what は「〜するもの」、whatever は「〜するものはすべて」となります。

 Let's Listen!　　　　会話の大意を聞き取ろう！

ジャスティンとミナコの会話を聞いて、質問に対する答えとして最も適切なものを (A) 〜 (C) の中から1つ選びましょう。　　 2-08

Question 1　What does Minako say she has to do?

(A) Submit a report
(B) Finish an experiment
(C) Carry out an experiment

Question 2　What does she say about the exam week?

(A) It will start tomorrow.
(B) She has only one week left before it starts.
(C) It will continue until the end of this month.

Question 3　What does Justin suggest?

(A) Minako should study harder.
(B) Minako should take a break.
(C) They should study together.

Let's Check & Read Aloud!

音読してみよう！

1. スクリプトを見ながら会話をもう１度聞き、下線部に当てはまる表現を書き入れましょう。（下線部には単語が２つ入ります）
2. 内容を確認して、全文を音読してみましょう。
3. ジャスティンとミナコの役割をパートナーと一緒に演じてみましょう。

2-08

Let's Practice the Roleplay!

Justin's Role   Minako's Role

Justin and Minako talk at the student lounge.

| Justin | Hi, Minako. You seem really busy. Are you OK? |

| Minako | Hi, Justin. I'm fine, thanks. I just have ①＿＿＿＿＿＿＿＿＿ a report as soon as possible. |

| Justin | Uh-huh. ②＿＿＿＿＿＿＿＿＿ about? |

| Minako | Basic chemistry. The experiment was over yesterday, but putting the ③＿＿＿＿＿＿＿＿＿ a report is difficult. |

| Justin | Yeah, I see ④＿＿＿＿＿＿＿＿＿ mean. |

| Minako | Besides, it's only one week until the ⑤＿＿＿＿＿＿＿＿＿ , so I have to study for the exams. |

| Justin | Don't worry. They are not so difficult. ⑥＿＿＿＿＿＿＿＿＿ . |

| Minako | Really? |

| Justin | Yes, I'm positive. Why don't you take ⑦＿＿＿＿＿＿＿＿＿ ? How about having some ice cream? |

| Minako | Hmmm, maybe you're right. It's not good to work on an ⑧＿＿＿＿＿＿＿＿＿ ＿＿＿＿＿＿＿ . Let's go! |

 **音読のヒント**

the experiment の the をつい「ザ」[ðə] と言ってしまうかもしれませんが、母音で始まる単語の前にある the は「ジ」[ði] と発音します。ただし、unit のように、母音字 u で始まっていても実際の発音が母音で始まらない場合は「ザ」と発音します。例：the university [ðə jù:nəvə́:rsəti]
また、uh-huh は、「うん、ええ、そうですか」のように、同意やあいづちに使われる表現ですが、発音はなかなか難しいです。鼻にかけた感じの「アハァ」[əhʌ́] で、後の「ハァ」の部分は上がり調子になります。

A. 次の文の空所に補うのに適切な関係代名詞をカッコ内から選び○で囲みましょう。

1. An experiment is a scientific test (what / that / whose) you do in order to discover if something is true.

2. Fieldwork is research or study (who / whose / which) is done in the real world rather than in a laboratory.

3. Let me know (what / which / that) you need for the experiment.

4. The hydrogen engine is an idea (who / whose / which) time has come.

B. 例にならい、関係代名詞節を用いて2つの文を1つにまとめましょう。出だしが書いてあるものはそれに続く形で文を作りましょう。

例　Rob gave me a USB memory. I've lost it.
　　I've lost　the USB memory (that) Rob gave me.

1. Justin has a cousin. She lives in Spain.

　　_____

2. The website is very useful. You told me about it.
　　The website _____

3. Yesterday I met an American scientist. I can't remember his name.
　　Yesterday I met an American scientist _____

4. Rob is studying with a girl. Do you know the girl?
　　Do you know the girl _____

C. 日本語の意味に合うようにカッコ内の語句を並べ替え、英文を完成させましょう。ただし、文の始めにくる単語も小文字にしてあり、1つ余分な語句が含まれています。

1. 私の言いたいことがわかりますか？
　　Do (I / which / mean / what / know / you)?

　　_____

2. 私に何かお手伝いできることがありますか？
　　(anything / can do / is / there / I / are) to help?

　　_____

3. 私の書いたレポートを確認してもらえませんか？
　　Could you (report / wrote / check / I / what / the)?

　　_____

4. 水素は酸素と結びついて水を作り出す気体です。
　　Hydrogen is a gas (that / with oxygen / who / to / combines / form water).

　　_____

 **Let's Read!**

次のパッセージを読み、その内容について 1～3 の質問に答えましょう。　 2-09

Hydrogen

An element is a simple substance that you cannot reduce to smaller chemical parts. One such element is hydrogen (H). Hydrogen exists naturally as a molecule, consisting of two hydrogen atoms with the chemical formula H_2. It was named by Antoine Lavoisier, an 18th century French scientist. The name comes from the Greek "hydro" (water) and "genos" (forming).

Hydrogen could play an important role in helping to reduce greenhouse gas emissions. It can be burned in an engine or reacted with oxygen in a fuel cell. Both processes produce electricity which can power electric vehicles. Hydrogen cars produce one <u>harmless</u> exhaust gas—water vapor.

---

1. Which sentence is true?

   (A) The hydrogen element has the chemical formula H_2.

   (B) Hydrogen was named after a French scientist.

   (C) Hydrogen cannot be broken down into other substances.

2. According to the passage, hydrogen could _____ in helping to reduce greenhouse gas emissions.

   (A) not be given a key role

   (B) be very useful

   (C) play hardly any role

3. The underlined word "harmless" means _____ .

   (A) causing no damage

   (B) having no purpose

   (C) creating no value

📖 **Notes**

molecule: 分子　　　　　　　　　　　　　　chemical formula: 化学式

Antoine Lavoisier: アントワーヌ・ラヴォアジエ　　fuel cell: 燃料電池

exhaust gas: 排出ガス

Challenge Yourself!

Part I **Photographs**

(A)〜(C) の英文を聞き、写真の描写として最も適切なものを選びましょう。 🎧 2-10

1.

(A)　　(B)　　(C)

2.

(A)　　(B)　　(C)

Part II **Question-Response**

最初に聞こえてくる英文に対する応答として最も適切なものを（A）〜（C）の中 🎧 2-11
から選びましょう。

3. (A)　　(B)　　(C)

4. (A)　　(B)　　(C)

Part III **Short Conversations**

会話を聞き、下の英文が会話の内容と合っていれば T（True）、間違っていれば 🎧 2-12
F（False）を○で囲みましょう。

5. The man is studying hard for the tests.　　　　　　　　　T　　　F

6. The man would prefer to do an online class on Mondays.　T　　　F

 Let's Read Aloud & Write! 音読筆写で覚えよう！

授業のまとめとして、今日学習した対話文を3回書き写して
しっかり覚えましょう。1度英文を声に出して読んでから書き
写すと頭に残りやすくなります。

今日のまとめ

英語で答えられますか？　　Have you ever stayed up studying all night before an exam?

Unit 14 I'm worried about my English test.

期末試験中のある日、ミナコとロブは大学の正門近くで話をしています。会話では、感想を述べたり、不安を示したりする際の表現を学びます。また、文法では比較、読解では元素3（炭素）に焦点を当てて学習します。

 ## Warm-up

授業前に確認しておこう！

Vocabulary Preview

 2-13

1～10 の語句の意味として適切なものを a ～ j の中から選びましょう。

1. term	_____	a. 少なくとも
2. friction	_____	b. 覚える、暗記する
3. at least	_____	c. 上級の
4. memorize	_____	d. つらい、厳しい
5. tough	_____	e. 道具、工具
6. pass	_____	f. 合格する
7. over	_____	g. 用語
8. advanced	_____	h. 精神的に疲れる、緊張が多い
9. stressful	_____	i. 終わって
10. tool	_____	j. 摩擦

ビートに乗って 1～10 の語句を発音してみましょう。

Grammar Point : 比較

I'm **as busy as** a bee* during the test week. （試験週間中はとても忙しいです）

The final exam was **more difficult than** I thought.

（期末試験は思っていたよりも難しかったです）

I find Technical English **the most difficult** of all the subjects.

（私はすべての科目の中で技術英語が最も難しいと感じます）

＊ as busy as a bee:「働きバチと同じくらい忙しい」で「とても忙しい」という意味を表します。

　形容詞や副詞を使って「～と同じくらい…だ」と2つのものを比較する場合、≪ as ＋形容詞／副詞＋ as ... ≫という形で表します。

　また、「～より面白い」や「最も面白い」のように、他と比較しながら話す場合、「面白い」という形容詞の比較級や最上級を使って表現します。比較級や最上級にするには、「1 音節の短い単語は語尾に -er（比較級）、-est（最上級）をつけ、3 音節以上の長い単語は前に more（比較級）、most（最上級）をつける」が基本ですが、2 音節の単語は両方のパターンがあります。また、不規則に変化す

	1 音節	2 音節	3 音節
比較級	-er		more ～
最上級	-est		most ～

るものも多くあります。下の表を完成させながら確認しましょう。

音節については巻末資料を参照してください。

	原級	比較級	最上級	
1 音節	high	higher	highest	語尾に -er/-est をつける（基本パターン）
	large	larger	largest	語尾に -r/-st をつける（-e で終わる単語）
	big			子音字を重ねて -er/-est をつける（＜１母音字＋１子音字＞で終わる単語）
2 音節	early	earlier	earliest	y を i に変え -er/-est をつける（＜子音字＋y ＞で終わる単語）
	simple	simpler	simplest	語尾に -(e)r/-(e)st をつける（-er, -le, -ow で終わる単語）
3 音節以上	slowly*	more slowly	most slowly	前に more/most をつける（＊形容詞に -ly がついた副詞は前に more/most をつける）
	difficult	more difficult	most difficult	
	many/much	more	most	不規則な変化をする（例外的な単語）
	good/well			
	little			
	bad/badly/ill			

下の例文の日本語訳を完成させながら使い方を確認しましょう。

Don't worry. This experiment isn't **as difficult as** it seems.

（　　　　　　　　　　　　　　　　　　　　　　　　　　）

This is the **most exciting** experiment that I've ever done.

（　　　　　　　　　　　　　　　　　　　　　　　　　　）

 Let's Listen!　　　　　　　会話の大意を聞き取ろう！

ミナコとロブの会話を聞いて、質問に対する答えとして最も適切なものを(A)〜(C) 2-14
の中から１つ選びましょう。

Question 1　What does Rob say about his test?

(A) His score needs to be more than 60 percent.

(B) It wasn't as difficult as he thought.

(C) He's sure that he will pass.

Question 2　When will Minako take her English test?

(A) Today

(B) Tomorrow

(C) The day after tomorrow

Question 3　What does she say about her test?

(A) She's prepared for it.

(B) She has to memorize a lot of facts.

(C) She has to learn technical terms.

Let's Check & Read Aloud!

音読してみよう！

1. ススクリプトを見ながら会話をもう1度聞き、下線部に当てはまる表現を書き 入れましょう。（下線部には単語が2つ入ります） 2-14
2. 内容を確認して、全文を音読してみましょう。
3. ミナコとロブの役割をパートナーと一緒に演じてみましょう。

Let's Practice the Roleplay!

Rob's Role   Minako's Role

Rob and Minako talk near the school entrance.

Rob Final ①＿＿＿＿＿＿＿＿ is so stressful!

Minako Yes, it sure is. I hope it will be ②＿＿＿＿＿＿＿＿ .

Rob I took my advanced Japanese final exam yesterday, and it was very difficult. In fact, it was the most difficult test ③＿＿＿＿＿＿＿＿ here.

Minako Oh, really? That's too bad.

Rob If I don't get over 60 percent, I ④＿＿＿＿＿＿＿＿ . So I'm really worried.

Minako Don't worry. I'm sure you'll pass. Besides, ⑤＿＿＿＿＿＿＿＿ it's over. I'm worried about my English test tomorrow.

Rob Why? Your English is excellent.

Minako Thanks. But it's ⑥＿＿＿＿＿＿＿＿ English, so the vocabulary is very difficult. I have ⑦＿＿＿＿＿＿＿＿ more than a hundred technical terms.

Rob Wow! ⑧＿＿＿＿＿＿＿＿ !

Minako Yes, but I'll try my best.

 音読のヒント

will not の短縮形 won't [wóʊnt]「ウォゥント」は、want [wánt / wɔ́nt]「ワント／ウォント」と発音が 似ており、区別が難しいものです。won't を発音する際は [oʊ] の部分を少し強調するようにすればよ いでしょう。また、won't など否定を表す語は、一般に文の中で強勢を入れて<u>強く、はっきりと、長 めに</u>発音されますのでその点にも注意しましょう。

Grammar

A. 例にならい、空所に下線部の単語の比較級か最上級を入れて次の1～4の文を完成させましょう。

例 I can't speak Japanese very <u>well</u>. Justin speaks it (*better*) than me.

1. Biology class is very <u>exciting</u>. It's the (　　　　　　　) class I've ever had.

2. Quality is very <u>important</u>. It's (　　　　　　) than quantity.

3. Today's exam was very <u>easy</u>. It was (　　　　　　) than the one I took yesterday.

4. This factory is very <u>large</u>. In fact, it's the (　　　　　　) factory in Ohio.

B. 例にならい、カッコ内から正しい語句を選び○で囲みましょう。

例 Rob is the tallest ((in) / from) our club.

1. Sarah is the same age (as / than) Minako.

2. This tool is (two / twice) as heavy as that one.

3. Justin studies (much / very) harder than me.

4. Basic chemistry is the most popular (in / of) all the subjects.

C. 日本語の意味に合うようにカッコ内の語句を並べ替え、英文を完成させましょう。ただし、文の始めにくる単語も小文字にしてあり、<u>1つ余分な語句が含まれています</u>。

1. 実験は思ったほど難しくありませんでした。
   The experiment (as / thought / more / difficult / as I / wasn't).

   _____

2. フィールドワークは通常の授業よりはるかに人気があります。
   Fieldwork (more / than / popular / is / better / much) regular classes.

   _____

3. どの科目が1番好きですか？
   Which (do / subject / the best / better / you / like)?

   _____

4. それは今まで受けた中で最も難しい試験でした。
   It was (exam / the / hardest / taken / I've ever / most).

   _____

 **Let's Read!**

読解力を高めよう！

次のパッセージを読み、その内容について 1〜3 の質問に答えましょう。　　 2-15

How Much Carbon Are We?

Carbon is an interesting element. In nature, it is found in two forms: diamonds and graphite. Diamonds are the hardest natural substance, so they are often used to make cutting tools. Of course, diamonds are also popular gemstones. Graphite, on the other hand, is soft, dark and gray. It is used in the middle of pencils, and often to reduce friction in machine parts. Did you know that carbon can be found in all foods and every living thing? The human body is about 65% water, but about 12% of the body's atoms are carbon, and 50% of the dry mass of a human body is carbon.

---

1. According to the passage, both diamonds and graphite can be used for _____ .

    (A) industrial purposes

    (B) making jewelry

    (C) reducing friction

2. Which sentence is true?

    (A) The appearance of graphite is quite similar to a diamond.

    (B) Graphite often produces friction in machine parts.

    (C) Carbon exists in all foods and every living thing.

3. When all the water has been removed from a human body, what percentage of the remains is carbon?

    (A) 12%

    (B) 50%

    (C) 65%

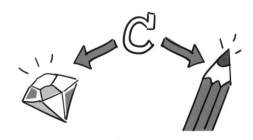

 Notes

graphite: 黒鉛　　　　　　on the other hand: 一方、それに対して

dry mass: 乾燥質量

Challenge Yourself!

リスニング力を試そう！

Part I **Photographs**

（A）〜（C）の英文を聞き、写真の描写として最も適切なものを選びましょう。  2-16

1.

(A) (B) (C)

2.

(A) (B) (C)

Part II **Question-Response**

最初に聞こえてくる英文に対する応答として最も適切なものを（A）〜（C）の中から選びましょう。 2-17

3. (A)   (B)   (C)

4. (A)   (B)   (C)

Part III **Short Conversations**

会話を聞き、下の英文が会話の内容と合っていれば T（True）、間違っていれば F（False）を○で囲みましょう。 2-18

5. The man and woman see few benefits in learning English.   T   F

6. The woman doesn't think she'll do well on the test.   T   F

 Let's Read Aloud & Write!

音読筆写で覚えよう！

授業のまとめとして、今日学習した対話文を3回書き写してしっかり覚えましょう。1度英文を声に出して読んでから書き写すと頭に残りやすくなります。

┤ **今日のまとめ** ├─

英語で答えられますか？   What is the most difficult subject for you?

Unit 15 Do you have any plans?

文法 ▶ 接続詞・前置詞

試験週間がもうじき終わるある日、ミナコとジャス
ティンは学生食堂で長期休暇の話をします。会話では、
予定を述べたり、賛同したりする際の表現を学びます。
また、文法では**接続詞・前置詞**、読解では**代替エネル
ギー**に焦点を当てて学習します。

 Warm-up　　　　　　　　　授業前に確認しておこう！

Vocabulary Preview
 2-19

1〜10 の語句の意味として適切なものを a 〜 j の中から選びましょう。

1. specific	＿＿＿＿	a. バイク
2. dormitory	＿＿＿＿	b. 持続可能な
3. as far as	＿＿＿＿	c. 地球温暖化
4. motorcycle	＿＿＿＿	d. 汚染
5. sustainable	＿＿＿＿	e. 〜に参加する
6. renewable	＿＿＿＿	f. 特定の
7. pollution	＿＿＿＿	g. 寮
8. take part in	＿＿＿＿	h. 〜まで、〜の所まで
9. geothermal	＿＿＿＿	i. 地熱の
10. global warming	＿＿＿＿	j. 再生可能な

ビートに乗って 1〜10 の語句を発音してみましょう。

Grammar Point : 接続詞・前置詞

<u>If</u> you like, why don't you join our research group?

（もしよければ私たちの研究グループに入りませんか？）

I'll go on a trip <u>as soon as</u> school is over.

（学校が終わったらすぐに旅行に出かけるつもりです）

Most of the fieldwork was carried out <u>in</u> Seoul.

（フィールドワークの大半はソウルで行われました）

　<u>接続詞</u>は様々な語や<u>句</u>、<u>節</u>などを結びつける役割を果たします。because や if のようによく知ら
れたものの他、as soon as（〜したらすぐに）などのように 2 語以上で接続詞
的に使われるものもあります。次の表に枠の中から適切な接続詞を書き入れて
確認しましょう。

because	〜なので	after	〜した後で		〜しなければ
or	または	before	〜する前に		〜だけれども
so	それで	when	〜するとき		〜の場合は
	〜の間		〜するまで		〜である限りは

because ✓
although
as long as
in case
while
until
unless

次に、**前置詞**は、**in** August や **on** Sunday morning のように、名詞や名詞句の前に置かれ、形容詞や副詞の役割を果たします。前置詞と名詞が一緒になったものを**前置詞句**と呼びます。

接続詞と前置詞では、because と because of、while と during など、意味の似たものがありますので違いを確認しておきましょう。接続詞と前置詞を見分けるポイントは次の通りです。

接続詞	その後に主語と動詞を含む語句（＝**節**）が続く。 ex.) I want to research this <u>because</u> I like fieldwork.
前置詞	その後に主語と動詞を含まない語句（＝**句**）が続く。 ex.) The fieldwork was put off <u>because of</u> heavy rain.

下の例文の日本語訳を完成させながら使い方を確認しましょう。

I'll be staying in Seoul <u>during</u> the fieldwork.

（　　　　　　　　　　　　　　　　　　　　　　）

I lost my laptop <u>while</u> (I was) doing the fieldwork.

（　　　　　　　　　　　　　　　　　　　　　　）

Let's Listen!

会話の大意を聞き取ろう！

ミナコとジャスティンの会話を聞いて、質問に対する答えとして最も適切なものを
(A)～(C) の中から1つ選びましょう。 2-20

Question 1 How is Justin going to spend his vacation?

(A) He's going back to his hometown.
(B) He's going to travel around Japan alone.
(C) He's going on a trip with Rob.

Question 2 What is Minako's plan for her vacation?

(A) She'll join a language program.
(B) She'll travel by motorcycle.
(C) She'll take part in a volunteer program.

Question 3 Is she going to stay in a dormitory?

(A) Yes, she is.
(B) No, she isn't.
(C) She hasn't decided yet.

Let's Check & Read Aloud!

1. スクリプトを見ながら会話をもう１度聞き、下線部に当てはまる表現を書き入れましょう。（下線部には単語が２つ入ります） 2-20
2. 内容を確認して、全文を音読してみましょう。
3. ミナコとジャスティンの役割をパートナーと一緒に演じてみましょう。

Let's Practice the Roleplay!

Minako's Role   Justin's Role

Minako and Justin talk at the school cafeteria.

Minako	The summer vacation is ①_____ the corner. Do you have any plans?
Justin	Yes, Rob and I are planning to ②_____ Japan during the summer vacation.
Minako	Sounds like a lot of fun. Do you have ③_____ plans?
Justin	Yeah, we're going as far as Kyushu by motorcycle this time, so it's ④_____ _____ be a long trip. How about you?
Minako	I'm going to take ⑤_____ the summer English program at your university in Ohio!
Justin	Wow, that's nice! How long are you going to stay there?
Minako	For ⑥_____ .
Justin	Are you going to stay in a dormitory?
Minako	No, I'll ⑦_____ with a host family.
Justin	Well, ⑧_____ have a very exciting vacation.
Minako	Yeah, that's for sure.

💡 **聞き取りのヒント**

実際の会話では、going to（〜するつもり）という表現は、「ゴーイング・トゥ」ではなく、「ゴーイントゥ」や [gənə, gɔ́nə]「ガナ、ゴナ」と１語のように聞こえることがよくあります。また、スクリプトでも実際の発音通りにgonnaと１語に綴られることが多くあります。このように音が変化してしまう例は、他にも want to（〜したい）⇒ wanna [wʌ́nə, wɔ́nə]「ワナ、ウォナ」がよく知られています。なお、gonna や wanna などは略式の表記方法ですから、英文を書く際には going to、want to と書くようにしましょう。

A. 例にならい、枠の中から適切な単語を選んで次の1〜4の文を完成させましょう。

例 My computer freezes all the time, (so) I need to buy a new one.

1. You can join our project (　　　　) you like.

2. You won't pass your examinations (　　　　) you study hard.

3. I'm tired, (　　　　) I have to finish this report.

4. Hurry up, (　　　　) we'll be late for the experiment!

or
if
unless
so ✓
but

B. 例にならい、カッコ内から正しい語句を選び○で囲みましょう。

例 I came home (at / on) nine o'clock.

1. I'm planning to study abroad (while / during) the summer vacation.

2. Rob goes to school (by / with) motorcycle.

3. Justin was late for class (because / because of) he was caught in a traffic jam.

4. The laboratory is (on / at) the third floor.

C. 日本語の意味に合うようにカッコ内の語句を並べ替え、英文を完成させましょう。ただし、文の始めにくる単語も小文字にしてあり、1つ余分な語句が含まれています。

1. 私はある調査研究に参加する予定です。
   I'm planning (in / a / take / with / to / part) research study.

   _____

2. ホームステイの予定ですか？
   Are (to / stay / going / you / on / with) a host family?

   _____

3. フィールドワークはもうじきです。
   (corner / fieldwork / the / until / around / is just).

   _____

4. 私たちは学校が終わったらすぐに旅行に行きます。
   We'll go (trip / so / a / as / on / soon) as school is over.

   _____

Let's Read!

次のパッセージを読み、その内容について 1～3 の質問に答えましょう。 2-21

Could you become a Superhero?

The superheroes of the 20th century often took the form of men with capes, fancy costumes and superhuman powers. The superheroes of the 21st century will look very different. They'll be the women and men in white lab coats with the superpower to save the planet from global warming. They'll research and create ways to produce sustainable and renewable energy.

Can you imagine making your mark in history as "Wind Power Woman," "Solar Man," "Geothermal Girl" or "Biomass Boy"? Or maybe your superpower will be to develop new fuel cells, or end plastic pollution? However you make a difference, let's try to make it a good one.

---

1. This passage suggests that _____ will save our planet.

   (A) scientists, rather than traditional superheroes,

   (B) only scientists who wear capes and fancy costumes

   (C) those who are interested in developing superhuman powers

2. Which sentence is true?

   (A) "Wind Power Woman" is an example of a traditional superhero.

   (B) Typical superheroes used to be men with capes, fancy costumes and superhuman powers.

   (C) The superheroes of the 21st century will be similar to those of the 20th century.

3. The underlined phrase "making your mark in history" means _____ .

   (A) being remembered for your success in your profession

   (B) getting good marks in the history exam

   (C) writing articles on the history of science

📖 **Notes**

fancy: 派手な　　　　biomass: バイオマス（代替エネルギーの供給源としての植物）

Challenge Yourself!

Part I Photographs

(A) ～ (C) の英文を聞き、写真の描写として最も適切なものを選びましょう。　 2-22

1.

(A)　　　(B)　　　(C)

2.

(A)　　　(B)　　　(C)

Part II Question-Response

最初に聞こえてくる英文に対する応答として最も適切なものを（A）～（C）の中から選びましょう。　　2-23

3.　(A)　　　(B)　　　(C)

4.　(A)　　　(B)　　　(C)

Part III Short Conversations

会話を聞き、下の英文が会話の内容と合っていれば T（True）、間違っていれば F（False）を○で囲みましょう。　　2-24

5. The woman will enjoy her vacation at the science museum.　　　T　　　F

6. The woman has been to Malaysia.　　　T　　　F

 Let's Read Aloud & Write!

授業のまとめとして、今日学習した対話文を3回書き写してしっかり覚えましょう。1度英文を声に出して読んでから書き写すと頭に残りやすくなります。

┌─ **今日のまとめ** ─┐

英語で答えられますか？　　What are you going to do during the summer vacation?

97

Let's Review

 Unit 01 Let's Review!　　　しっかり復習しよう！

Quick Response Training   2-25

1. 日本語の文と同じ意味を表すようにカッコ内に適切な単語を入れて英文を完成させましょう。
2. 日本語の文を見てすぐさま対応する英文が言えるように繰り返し練習しましょう。英文の箇所を隠して練習すると効果的です。
3. 1〜10 までの日本語の文を何秒で英文にして言えるかペアで競い合ってみましょう。

Your Time ⏱ ＿＿＿＿＿ seconds

1. 私の専攻は工学です。	1. My major (　　　　) engineering.
2. 私たちは同じ英語のクラスです。	2. We (　　　　) in the same English class.
3. 工学は彼の専攻ではありません。	3. Engineering (　　　　) his major.
4. 日本に来るのはこれが初めてですか？	4. (　　　　) this your first visit to Japan?
5. 私は生物学を専攻しているのではありません。	5. I'm (　　　　) a biology major.
6. あなたは生物学科ですか？	6. (　　　　) you in the biology department?
7. あなたの専攻は何ですか？	7. (　　　　) is your major?
8. 先生はどこにいるのですか？	8. (　　　　) is the teacher?
9. 期末試験はいつですか？	9. (　　　　) is the final exam?
10. 太陽系にはいくつの惑星がありますか？	10. How (　　　　) planets are there in the solar system?

TESTUDY Training

　授業の復習として、テスタディの問題を解いておきましょう。
次回授業の始めに復習テストがあります。

Quick Response Training

 2-26

1. 日本語の文と同じ意味を表すようにカッコ内に適切な単語を入れて英文を完成させましょう。
2. 日本語の文を見てすぐさま対応する英文が言えるように繰り返し練習しましょう。英文の箇所を隠して練習すると効果的です。
3. 1～10までの日本語の文を何秒で英文にして言えるかペアで競い合ってみましょう。

Your Time 🕐 _____ seconds

1. 私たちは科学クラブに所属しています。	1. We（　　　　）to the science club.
2. サラも科学クラブに所属しています。	2. Sarah（　　　　）to the science club, too.
3. 父は高校で数学を教えています。	3. My father（　　　　）math at a high school.
4. 新しい学校は気に入っていますか？	4. （　　　　）you like your new school?
5. 彼は車の運転をするのですか？	5. （　　　　）he drive?
6. 私は運転免許証を持っていません。	6. I（　　　　）have a driver's license.
7. 兄も運転免許証は持っていません。	7. My brother（　　　　）have a driver's license, either. ＊ either と too はどちらも「～も」という意味ですが、肯定文では too を使い、否定文では either を使います。
8. お仕事は何ですか？	8. What（　　　　）you do（for a living）?
9. 私は大学生です。	9. （　　　　）a college student.
10. 日本はいかがですか？	10. （　　　　）do you like Japan?

TESTUDY Training

授業の復習として、テスタディの問題を解いておきましょう。
次回授業の始めに復習テストがあります。

Unit 03 **Let's Review!**

Quick Response Training

  2-27

1. 日本語の文と同じ意味を表すようにカッコ内に適切な単語を入れて英文を完成させましょう。
2. 日本語の文を見てすぐさま対応する英文が言えるように繰り返し練習しましょう。英文の箇所を隠して練習すると効果的です。
3. 1～10 までの日本語の文を何秒で英文にして言えるかペアで競い合ってみましょう。

Your Time 🕐 _____ **seconds**

1. 私は一人暮らしをしたかったのです。	1. I ( ) to live alone.
2. 数学クラブに入りましたか？	2. ( ) you join the mathematics club?
3. いいえ、私はどのクラブにも入りませんでした。	3. No, I ( ) join any club.
4. 父は生物学を専攻しました。	4. My father ( ) in biology.
5. お母さんも生物学を専攻されたのですか？	5. ( ) your mother major in biology, too?
6. いいえ、彼女は大学には行きませんでした。	6. No, she ( ) go to college.
7. ロブはいつ日本に来ましたか？	7. ( ) did Rob come to Japan?
8. 彼は8ヵ月前ここに来ました。	8. He ( ) here eight months ago.
9. このクラブはどれくらいの頻度で会いますか？	9. How ( ) does this club meet?
10. 私たちは週に2回会います。	10. We meet ( ) a week.

TESTUDY Training

授業の復習として、テスタディの問題を解いておきましょう。
次回授業の始めに復習テストがあります。

Unit 04 Let's Review! しっかり復習しよう！

Quick Response Training 2-28

1. 日本語の文と同じ意味を表すようにカッコ内に適切な単語を入れて英文を完成させましょう。
2. 日本語の文を見てすぐさま対応する英文が言えるように繰り返し練習しましょう。英文の箇所を隠して練習すると効果的です。
3. 1〜10までの日本語の文を何秒で英文にして言えるかペアで競い合ってみましょう。

Your Time 🕐 _____ seconds

1. 今、何をしているのですか？	1. What are you （　　　　　）?
2. （1人の）高校生に数学を教えているところです。	2. I'm （　　　　　） mathematics to a high school student.
3. アルバイトを探しているのですか？	3. Are you （　　　　　） for a part-time job?
4. いいえ、（私は）勉強に忙しいです。	4. No, （　　　　　） busy with my studies.
5. （あなたは）放課後に働いているのですか？	5. （　　　　　） you work after school?
6. はい、火曜と金曜の夕方に働いています。	6. Yes, I （　　　　　） on Tuesday and Friday evenings.
7. 電話してくれた時、私は仕事中でした。	7. I （　　　　　） working when you called me.
8. 今は仕事中ではありません。	8. I'm （　　　　　） working now.
9. 今朝起きた時、雪は降っていませんでした。	9. It （　　　　　） snowing when I got up this morning.
10. 私たちはあなたを信じています。	10. We （　　　　　） in you.

TESTUDY Training

授業の復習として、テスタディの問題を解いておきましょう。
次回授業の始めに復習テストがあります。

Unit 05 Let's Review!

しっかり復習しよう！

  2-29

Quick Response Training

1. 日本語の文と同じ意味を表すようにカッコ内に適切な単語を入れて英文を完成させましょう。
2. 日本語の文を見てすぐさま対応する英文が言えるように繰り返し練習しましょう。英文の箇所を隠して練習すると効果的です。
3. 1～10 までの日本語の文を何秒で英文にして言えるかペアで競い合ってみましょう。

Your Time 🕐 _____ seconds

1.【席を外す際に】すぐに戻ります。	1.（　　　　）be right back.
2.【席を外す際に】長くはかかりません（すぐに戻ります）。	2. I（　　　　）be long.
3. この週末は何をする予定ですか？	3. What（　　　　）you going to do this weekend?
4. プレゼンの準備をする予定です。	4. I'm going（　　　　）prepare for my presentation.
5. インターンシップに申し込む予定ですか？	5.（　　　　）you going to apply for an internship?
6. 平日にアルバイトをするつもりはありません。	6. I'm（　　　　）going to work part-time on weekdays.
7. 誰がグループリーダーになるでしょうか？	7. Who（　　　　）be the group leader?
8. 実験は正午までには終わるでしょう。	8. The experiment（　　　　）be over by noon.
9. それまであなたに電話できないでしょう。	9. I（　　　　）be able to call you until then.
10. 実験が終わるまで私は待っています。	10. I'll be waiting until the experiment（　　　　）over.

TESTUDY Training

授業の復習として、テスタディの問題を解いておきましょう。
次回授業の始めに復習テストがあります。

102

Unit 06 Let's Review!

しっかり復習しよう！

Quick Response Training

 2-30

1. 日本語の文と同じ意味を表すようにカッコ内に適切な単語を入れて英文を完成させましょう。
2. 日本語の文を見てすぐさま対応する英文が言えるように繰り返し練習しましょう。英文の箇所を隠して練習すると効果的です。
3. 1～10までの日本語の文を何秒で英文にして言えるかペアで競い合ってみましょう。

Your Time 🕐 _____ **seconds**

1. きっとお疲れでしょう（あなたは疲れているに違いありません）。	1. You （　　　　） be tired.
2. お手洗いに行ってもいいですか？	2. Can*1 I （　　　　） excused?
3. お手洗いはどこでしょうか（私はどこで手を洗うことができますか）？	3. Where can （　　　　） wash my hands?
4. このレポートを見ていただけませんか？	4. Could*2 （　　　　） take a look at this report?
5. 私はこのレポートを今日提出しなければなりません。	5. I have （　　　　） submit this report today.
6. 今日それを提出する必要はありません。	6. You （　　　　） have to submit it today.
7. 【レストランで】4人用の席をお願いします。	7. I'd*3 （　　　　） a table for four, please.
8. お聞きしたいことがあるのですが。	8. I'd like （　　　　） ask you a question.
9. 私は間違っているかもしれません。	9. I may*4 （　　　　） wrong.
10. 私は以前、この近くに住んでいました。	10. I used （　　　　） live near here.

[NOTES]
1. may や could を使うことも可能です。
2. can も可能ですが、could を使うと丁寧な感じになります。
3. 連れの人のことを意識して We'd ということも可能です。
4. might を使うことも可能です。

TESTUDY Training

授業の復習として、テスタディの問題を解いておきましょう。
次回授業の始めに復習テストがあります。

Unit 07 Let's Review!　　　　　　　しっかり復習しよう！

Quick Response Training　　 2-31

1. 日本語の文と同じ意味を表すようにカッコ内に適切な単語を入れて英文を完成させましょう。
2. 日本語の文を見てすぐさま対応する英文が言えるように繰り返し練習しましょう。英文の箇所を隠して練習すると効果的です。
3. 1〜10までの日本語の文を何秒で英文にして言えるかペアで競い合ってみましょう。

Your Time 🕐 _____ seconds

1. このプロジェクトはレボリューションと呼ばれています。	1. This project (　　　　　) called Revolution.
2. それはあるロックバンドの名前にちなんで名づけられました。	2. It (　　　　　) named after the name of a rock band.
3. あなたがそのプロジェクトのリーダーになったのですか？	3. Did you (　　　　　) the leader of the project?
4. いいえ、私は選ばれませんでした。	4. No, I (　　　　　) chosen.
5. 誰が選ばれたのですか？	5. Who (　　　　　) chosen?
6. 次の会議はいつ行われるのですか？	6. When (　　　　　) the next meeting be held?
7. 次の会議は今週行われなければなりません。	7. The next meeting (　　　　　) to be held this week.
8. これを英語で何と呼びますか？	8. What (　　　　　) you call this in English?
9. これは英語で何と呼ばれていますか？	9. What is this (　　　　　) in English?
10. 私のノートパソコンは現在、修理中です。	10. My laptop is (　　　　　) repaired now.

TESTUDY Training

授業の復習として、テスタディの問題を解いておきましょう。次回授業の始めに復習テストがあります。

Unit 08 Let's Review!

しっかり復習しよう！

Quick Response Training

 2-32

1. 日本語の文と同じ意味を表すようにカッコ内に適切な単語を入れて英文を完成させましょう。
2. 日本語の文を見てすぐさま対応する英文が言えるように繰り返し練習しましょう。英文の箇所を隠して練習すると効果的です。
3. 1〜10 までの日本語の文を何秒で英文にして言えるかペアで競い合ってみましょう。

Your Time 🕐 _____ seconds

1. （私は）先月 3 日間入院しました。	1. I (　　　　) in the hospital for three days last month.
2. （私は）入院して 3 日になります。	2. (　　　　) been in the hospital for three days.
3. あなたはいつその科目を取りましたか？	3. When (　　　　) you take the subject?
4. あなたはもうその科目を取りましたか？	4. Have you (　　　　) the subject yet?
5. 今日はまだ薬を飲んでいません。	5. I (　　　　) taken my medicine yet today.
6. ロブは月曜日からずっと欠席しています。	6. Rob has been absent (　　　　) Monday.
7. 今までにフィールドワークをしたことがありますか？	7. Have you (　　　　) done any fieldwork?
8. 私たちはすでにフィールドワークを終えました。	8. We've (　　　　) finished our fieldwork.
9. 私たちはまだフィールドワークをしたことがありません。	9. We (　　　　) done any fieldwork yet.
10. 私は 1 度もフィールドワークをしたことがありません。	10. I've (　　　　) done any fieldwork.

TESTUDY Training

授業の復習として、テスタディの問題を解いておきましょう。
次回授業の始めに復習テストがあります。

Unit 09 Let's Review!

しっかり復習しよう！

 2-33

Quick Response Training

1. 日本語の文と同じ意味を表すようにカッコ内に適切な単語を入れて英文を完成させましょう。
2. 日本語の文を見てすぐさま対応する英文が言えるように繰り返し練習しましょう。英文の箇所を隠して練習すると効果的です。
3. 1〜10 までの日本語の文を何秒で英文にして言えるかペアで競い合ってみましょう。

Your Time ⏱ _____ seconds

1. ここで電話を使っても大丈夫ですか？	1. Is it OK （　　　　） use my phone here?
2. このプロジェクトを終了させるために協力しましょう。	2. Let's work together in （　　　　） to finish this project.
3. あなたにお願いがあります。	3. I have a favor to （　　　　） you.
4. 疲れすぎていて今夜は勉強できません。	4. I'm （　　　　） tired to study tonight.
5. サラは親切にも私を手伝ってくれました。	5. Sarah was kind （　　　　） to help me.
6. サラにデータの確認をしてもらうよう頼みましょう。	6. Let's （　　　　） Sarah to check the data.
7. お邪魔してすみませんが、手伝っていただけませんか？	7. I'm sorry （　　　　） bother you, but could you help me?
8. 私に何をしてほしいのですか？	8. What do you want （　　　　） to do?
9. どうしたらいいのかわかりません（何をしたらよいのかわかりません）。	9. I don't know （　　　　） to do.
10. この機器の使い方を教えてもらえませんか？	10. Could you tell me （　　　　） to use this equipment?

TESTUDY Training

授業の復習として、テスタディの問題を解いておきましょう。
次回授業の始めに復習テストがあります。

 **Let's Review!**

しっかり復習しよう！

Quick Response Training

 2-34

1. 日本語の文と同じ意味を表すようにカッコ内に適切な単語を入れて英文を完成させましょう。
2. 日本語の文を見てすぐさま対応する英文が言えるように繰り返し練習しましょう。英文の箇所を隠して練習すると効果的です。
3. 1〜10までの日本語の文を何秒で英文にして言えるかペアで競い合ってみましょう。

Your Time 🕐 _____ seconds

1. 実験室には人がほとんどいませんでした。	1. There were (　　　　　) people in the laboratory.
2. 残り時間はほとんどありません。	2. There's (　　　　　) time left.
3. もう少し時間をください。	3. Give me a (　　　　　) more time.
4. 私たちはもう数日必要です。	4. We need a (　　　　　) more days.
5. ジャスティンはよくレポートを提出し忘れます。	5. Justin (　　　　　) forgets to submit his reports.
6. 私たちはもう少しで締め切りに遅れるところでした。	6. We (　　　　　) missed the deadline.
7. ミナコは決して締め切りに遅れることはありません。	7. Minako (　　　　　) misses the deadline.
8. サラはグラフを作るのが得意です。	8. Sarah is (　　　　　) at making graphs.
9. 私はかろうじてその試験に合格しました。	9. I (　　　　　) passed the exam.
10. 火の取り扱いに注意しなければいけません（火に関して注意深くなければなりません）。	10. You have to be (　　　　　) with fire.

TESTUDY Training

授業の復習として、テスタディの問題を解いておきましょう。
次回授業の始めに復習テストがあります。

Quick Response Training

  2-35

1. 日本語の文と同じ意味を表すようにカッコ内に適切な単語を入れて英文を完成させましょう。
2. 日本語の文を見てすぐさま対応する英文が言えるように繰り返し練習しましょう。英文の箇所を隠して練習すると効果的です。
3. 1〜10までの日本語の文を何秒で英文にして言えるかペアで競い合ってみましょう。

Your Time 🕐 _____ **seconds**

1.（あなたは）退屈なのですか？	1. Are you（　　　　　）?
2. その新しいアプリは本当に退屈でした。	2. The new app was really（　　　　）.
3. 私はアプリ開発に興味があります。	3. I'm（　　　　）in app development.
4. 化学はとても興味深い科学分野です。	4. Chemistry is a very（　　　　）field of science.
5. お待たせしてすみませんでした。	5. I'm sorry to keep you（　　　　）.
6. 失われたデータは復元されました。	6. The（　　　　）data was restored.
7. データはサラに確認してもらいます。	7. I'll have the data（　　　　）by Sarah.
8. 期末試験まで後２日しか残されていません。	8. We have only two days（　　　　） before the final exam.
9. ドアの前に立っている男性を知っていますか？	9. Do you know the man（　　　　）in front of the door?
10. 実験用白衣を着ている女性は誰ですか？	10. Who is the woman（　　　　）a lab coat?

TESTUDY Training

授業の復習として、テスタディの問題を解いておきましょう。
次回授業の始めに復習テストがあります。

Unit 12 — Let's Review!

しっかり復習しよう！

Quick Response Training

 2-36

1. 日本語の文と同じ意味を表すようにカッコ内に適切な単語を入れて英文を完成させましょう。
2. 日本語の文を見てすぐさま対応する英文が言えるように繰り返し練習しましょう。英文の箇所を隠して練習すると効果的です。
3. 1〜10までの日本語の文を何秒で英文にして言えるかペアで競い合ってみましょう。

Your Time ⏰ _____ seconds

1. 私は英語を上手に話したいです。	1. I want to (　　　　　) English well.
2. 私は英語を話すことに慣れていません。	2. I'm not used (　　　　　) speaking English.
3. 私はもっと英語を話す練習をする必要があります。	3. I need to practice (　　　　　) English more.
4. 留学は外国語を学ぶのに良い方法です。	4. (　　　　　) abroad is a good way to learn a foreign language.
5. オンライン英会話を受けるのはどうですか？	5. How (　　　　　) taking online English conversation lessons?
6. オンライン英会話を受けることを考えています。	6. I'm thinking of (　　　　　) online English conversation lessons.
7. 返事が遅くなってすみません。	7. I'm sorry for (　　　　　) writing to you sooner.
8. この研究所を訪れたことは決して忘れません。	8. I'll never forget (　　　　　) this laboratory.
9. 忘れずに私に電話してください。	9. Don't forget (　　　　　) call me.
10. あなたにまたお会いできるのを楽しみにしています。	10. I'm looking forward (　　　　　) seeing you again.

TESTUDY Training

授業の復習として、テスタディの問題を解いておきましょう。
次回授業の始めに復習テストがあります。

Let's Review!

しっかり復習しよう！

Quick Response Training

 2-37

1. 日本語の文と同じ意味を表すようにカッコ内に適切な単語を入れて英文を完成させましょう。
2. 日本語の文を見てすぐさま対応する英文が言えるように繰り返し練習しましょう。英文の箇所を隠して練習すると効果的です。
3. 1〜10までの日本語の文を何秒で英文にして言えるかペアで競い合ってみましょう。

Your Time 🕐 _____ seconds

1. 私たちはこの実験を手伝ってくれる人が必要です。	1. We need someone that*1 can (　　　　　) with this experiment.
2. 私には化学に詳しい友人がいます。	2. I have a friend (　　　　　) knows a lot about chemistry.
3. 私たちには、明日提出する数学の宿題があります。	3. We have math homework that*2 (　　　　　) due tomorrow.
4. 娘さんがトーナメントで優勝した男性はプロのゴルファーです。	4. The man (　　　　　) daughter won the tournament is a professional golfer.
5. 何か私でお役に立てることはありますか？	5. Is (　　　　　) anything (that)*3 I can do to help?
6. 基礎物理は私が今まで受けた中で最も興味深い科目です。	6. Basic physics is the most interesting subject (　　　　　) I've ever taken.
7. スミス教授は私たちが知りたいことをすべて（私たちに）教えてくれます。	7. Professor Smith teaches us everything (　　　　　) we want to know.
8. あなたの言っていることはわかります。	8. I see (　　　　　) you mean.
9. それがあなたの知りたかったことですか？	9. Is that what (　　　　　) wanted to know?
10. 好きなものは何でも選んでいいですよ。	10. You can choose (　　　　　) you like. = anything (that)

[NOTES]
1. 先行詞が人で主格の場合、that も可能ですが、who を使うのが一般的です。
2. 先行詞が人以外で主格の場合、which も可能ですが that を使うのが一般的です。
3. 先行詞が目的格の場合省略することが多いですが、使うとすれば先行詞が人かどうかに関わらず that を使うのが一般的です。

TESTUDY Training

授業の復習として、テスタディの問題を解いておきましょう。
次回授業の始めに復習テストがあります。

Unit 14　Let's Review!

しっかり復習しよう！

 2-38

Quick Response Training

1. 日本語の文と同じ意味を表すようにカッコ内に適切な単語を入れて英文を完成させましょう。
2. 日本語の文を見てすぐさま対応する英文が言えるように繰り返し練習しましょう。英文の箇所を隠して練習すると効果的です。
3. 1～10までの日本語の文を何秒で英文にして言えるかペアで競い合ってみましょう。

Your Time 🕐 _____ **seconds**

1. その物質はダイアモンドと同じくらい硬いようです。	1. The substance seems as hard (　　　　　) diamond.
2. ダイヤモンドは他のどの物質より硬いです。	2. Diamond is (　　　　　) than any other substance.
3. 水素は空気より軽いです。	3. Hydrogen is lighter (　　　　　) air.
4. 最も軽い元素は何ですか？	4. What is (　　　　　) lightest element?
5. 水素が最も軽い元素です。	5. Hydrogen is the (　　　　　) element.
6. 2番目に軽い元素は何ですか？	6. What is the (　　　　　) lightest element?
7. ヘリウムが2番目に軽い元素です。	7. Helium is the second (　　　　　) element.
8. 基礎化学は予想していたより面白いです。	8. Basic chemistry is more fun (　　　　　) I expected.
9. 実験は予想していたほど面白くはありませんでした。	9. The experiment wasn't as much fun (　　　　　) I expected.
10. これは今まで経験した中で最も難しい実験です。	10. This is the (　　　　　) difficult experiment (that) I've ever experienced.

TESTUDY Training

　授業の復習として、テスタディの問題を解いておきましょう。
次回授業の始めに復習テストがあります。

Unit 15 Let's Review!

しっかり復習しよう！

Quick Response Training

 2-39

1. 日本語の文と同じ意味を表すようにカッコ内に適切な単語を入れて英文を完成させましょう。
2. 日本語の文を見てすぐさま対応する英文が言えるように繰り返し練習しましょう。英文の箇所を隠して練習すると効果的です。
3. 1～10 までの日本語の文を何秒で英文にして言えるかペアで競い合ってみましょう。

Your Time 🕐 _____ seconds

1. フィールドワークはソウルで行われました。	1. The fieldwork was carried out （　　　　） Seoul.
2. ジャスティンは午後に到着します。	2. Justin will arrive （　　　　） the afternoon.
3. サラは金曜日の午後に到着します。	3. Sarah will arrive （　　　　） Friday afternoon.
4. 夏休みの間に旅行に行くつもりです。	4. I'll go on a trip （　　　　） the summer vacation.
5. あなたが買い物をしている間、私はここにいます。	5. I'll be here （　　　　） you shop.
6. 正午にここで会いましょう。	6. Let's meet here （　　　　） noon.
7. 全員が戻ってくるまであなたはここにいなければいけません。	7. You have to be here （　　　　） everyone comes back.
8. 私たちは5時までにこのレポートを提出しなければいけません。	8. We have to hand in this report （　　　　） five o'clock.
9. 悪天候のために私たちの飛行機は遅れました。	9. Our plane was delayed because （　　　　） bad weather.
10. 試してみないと決してわかりませんよ。	10. You'll never know （　　　　） you try.

TESTUDY Training

授業の復習として、テスタディの問題を解いておきましょう。
次回授業の始めに復習テストがあります。

112

巻末資料

品詞の分類

名詞や動詞といった文法上の区分のことを**品詞**と言い、一般に下のように分類されます。

品 詞	働 き	例
名詞（Noun）	人や物事の名前を表す。	company, sale など
冠詞（Article）	名詞の前に置かれて、その単語が特定されるものかどうかを示す。	a, an, the
代名詞（Pronoun）	名詞の代わりをする。	I, my, me, mine など
動詞（Verb）	人や物事の状態や動作を表す。	want, keep, take など
助動詞（Auxiliary verb）	動詞と組み合わせて話し手の判断を示す。	can, will, must など
形容詞（Adjective）	人や物事の性質や状態などを表す。	big, beautiful など
副詞（Adverb）	動詞や形容詞、他の副詞などを修飾する。	really, always など
前置詞（Preposition）	名詞や名詞句の前に置かれ句を作る。	of, in, under, on など
接続詞（Conjunction）	語と語、句と句、節と節をつなぐ。	and, because, or など
間投詞（Interjection）	話し手の感情を表す。	oh, wow, ouch など

　単語は必ずしも1つの品詞でしか使われないわけではありません。意味のわからない単語を辞書で引く場合、その単語の品詞が何であるかをあらかじめ考えておくと、正しい意味に早くたどり着けるようになります。

文の要素と基本文型

英文を構成する要素には次のようなものがあります。

主語	文の中で「〜が、〜は」に当たるもの。	名詞、代名詞
述語動詞	文の中で「〜である」や「〜する」に当たるもの。	動詞
目的語	「〜を」や「〜に」など、動作の対象を示すもの。	名詞、代名詞
補語	主語や目的語が「どういうものか」もしくは「どんな状態なのか」を補足説明するもの。 ex. My name is Robert, but everyone calls me Rob. （私の名前はロバートですが、みんな私のことをロブと呼びます）	名詞、代名詞、形容詞
修飾語（句）	主語、述語動詞、目的語、補語に意味を付け加えるもの。 修飾語（句）を除いても文は成立します。 ex. I work for Sunrise Corporation. （私はサンライズ・コーポレーションに勤めています）	形容詞、副詞、前置詞句など

また、英文の基本文型としては下に挙げる**5文型**がよく知られています。

第1文型	SV （主語 + 動詞）	I cried.（私は泣きました）
第2文型	SVC （主語 + 動詞 + 補語）	My name is Robert. （私の名前はロバートです）
第3文型	SVO （主語 + 動詞 + 目的語）	I studied economics. （私は経済学を学びました）
第4文型	SVO_1O_2 （主語 + 動詞 + 目的語1 + 目的語2）	Julia gave me the report. （ジュリアが私にその報告書をくれました）
第5文型	SVOC （主語 + 動詞 + 目的語 + 補語）	Everybody calls me Rob. （みんな私のことをロブと呼びます）

　主語（Subject）、**述語動詞**（Verb）、**目的語**（Object）、**補語**（Complement）という基本要素の中で、目的語と補語の区別が文型を見分けるポイントになります。目的語は動詞が表す動作の対象を示し、補語は主語や目的語が「どういうものか」もしくは「どんな状態なのか」を補足説明するものです。ですから、第2文型と第3文型を見分ける場合、**「第2文型の場合 S ＝ C、第3文型の場合 S ≠ O」**という関係に着目するとよいでしょう。また、第4文型と第5文型を見分ける場合には、**「第4文型の場合 O_1 ≠ O_2、第5文型の場合 O ＝ C」**という関係が成り立つことに注意しておくことです。

▶ 人称代名詞の種類と格変化表

人称	数	主格 （～は）	所有格 （～の）	目的格 （～に、～を）	所有代名詞 （～のもの）	再帰代名詞 （～自身）
1人称	単数	I	my	me	mine	myself
	複数	we	our	us	ours	ourselves
2人称	単数	you	your	you	yours	yourself
	複数					yourselves
3人称	単数	he	his	him	his	himself
		she	her	her	hers	herself
		it	its	it	−	itself
	複数	they	their	them	theirs	themselves

不規則動詞変化表

	原　形	過去形	過去分詞	-ing 形	
A-A-A （原形、過去形、 過去分詞が すべて同じ）	cost cut hit put read	cost cut hit put read [réd]	cost cut hit put read [réd]	costing cutting hitting putting reading	（費用が）かかる 切る 叩く 置く 読む
A-B-A （原形と過去 分詞が同じ）	become come run	became came ran	become come run	becoming coming running	～になる 来る 走る
A-B-B （過去形と過去 分詞が同じ）	bring buy catch feel have hear keep leave make meet pay say send spend stand teach tell think understand	brought bought caught felt had heard kept left made met paid said sent spent stood taught told thought understood	brought bought caught felt had heard kept left made met paid said sent spent stood taught told thought understood	bringing buying catching feeling having hearing keeping leaving making meeting paying saying sending spending standing teaching telling thinking understanding	持ってくる 買う 捕まえる 感じる 持っている 聞く 保つ 立ち去る 作る 会う 払う 言う 送る 過ごす 立つ 教える 話す 思う 理解する
A-B-C （原形、過去形、 過去分詞が すべて異なる）	be begin break choose drink eat fall get give go know see speak take write	was/were began broke chose drank ate fell got gave went knew saw spoke took wrote	been begun broken chosen drunk eaten fallen gotten/got given gone known seen spoken taken written	being beginning breaking choosing drinking eating falling getting giving going knowing seeing speaking taking writing	～である 始まる 壊す 選ぶ 飲む 食べる 落ちる 手に入れる 与える 行く 知っている 見る 話す 取る 書く

▶ 音節

　音節とは、簡単に言うと、「母音を中心とした音のかたまり」で、[ái] といった二重母音も 1 つの母音と考えます。hot [hát] や big [bíg] などのごく短い単語は 1 音節ですが、strike [stráik] など、一見長そうに見える単語でも母音は [ái] しかありませんので、実は 1 音節です。

　単語が何音節であるかは、辞書に載っています。例えば、interesting を辞書で調べてみると、in・ter・est・ing のように区切られて表示されており、この区切りが音節の区切りを示しています。したがって、interesting は 4 音節だとわかります。

　慣れるまでは辞書で確かめるようにしてください。

▶発音記号の読み方① 母音編

■母音と子音

「母音」とは、日本語の「アイウエオ」のように、肺から出る空気が舌や歯、唇などに邪魔されずに自由に口から出る音のことです。これに対して、「子音」とは、喉から出る息や声が途中でいろいろと邪魔されて、口や鼻から出る音のことです。

■有声音と無声音

声帯が振動する音のことを「有声音」と言い、逆に声帯が振動しない音のことを「無声音」と言います。母音はすべて有声音ですが、子音には有声音と無声音の両方があります。

🎵 2-40, 41

短母音	[ɑ]	口を思いきり開け口の奥の方から「ア」。	box / hot
	[ʌ]	口をあまり開けない「ア」。	come / bus
	[ə]	口を軽く開けて弱く「ア」。	woman / about
	[æ]	「エ」の口の形で「ア」。	bank / hand
	[i]	日本語の「イ」と「エ」の中間。	sick / it
	[iː]	唇を左右に引いて「イー」。	see / chief
	[u]	[uː]よりも少し唇をゆるめて「ウ」。	good / look
	[uː]	唇を小さく丸めて「ウー」。	school / two
	[e]	日本語の「エ」とほぼ同じ。	net / desk
	[ɔː]	口を大きく開け唇を少し丸めて「オー」。	talk / ball
	[ɑːr]	口を大きく開けて「アー」の後、舌先を巻き上げた音を添える。	large / far
	[əːr]	口を軽く開けて「アー」の後、舌先を巻き上げた音を添える。	girl / work
二重母音	[ei]	始めの音を強く発音し、後の音は軽く添える感じで、「エィ」。	game / say
	[ɔi]	上と同じ感じで、「オィ」。	boy / oil
	[ai]	上と同じ感じで、「アィ」。	write / kind
	[au]	上と同じ感じで、「アゥ」。	house / now
	[ou]	上と同じ感じで、「オゥ」。	boat / cold
	[iər]	「イァ」に舌先を巻き上げた音を添える。	dear / hear
	[eər]	「エァ」に舌先を巻き上げた音を添える。	air / bear
	[uər]	「ウァ」に舌先を巻き上げた音を添える。	poor / tour

破裂音	[p]	「パ」行子音とほぼ同じ。		pen / cup
	[b]	[p]の有声音。「バ」行子音とほぼ同じ。		big / job
	[t]	「タ」行子音とほぼ同じ。		tea / meet
	[d]	[t]の有声音。「ダ」行子音とほぼ同じ。		day / food
	[k]	「カ」行子音とほぼ同じ。		cook / take
	[g]	[k]の有声音。「ガ」行子音とほぼ同じ。		game / leg
摩擦音	[f]	下唇を上の歯にあて、息を出して「フ」。		five / enough
	[v]	[f]の有声音で、「ヴ」。		voice / wave
	[θ]	舌先を前歯で軽く噛むようにして「ス」。		think / month
	[ð]	[θ]の有声音で、「ズ」。		there / brother
	[s]	「サ、ス、セ、ソ」の子音とほぼ同じ。		sea / nice
	[z]	[s]の有声音で、「ザ、ズ、ゼ、ゾ」の子音とほぼ同じ。		zoo / lose
	[ʃ]	「シ」とほぼ同じ。		she / fish
	[ʒ]	[ʃ]の有声音で、「ジ」。		usual / vision
	[h]	「ハー」と息を吹きかけてガラスを曇らせるときのような「ハ」。		hot / hand
破擦音	[tʃ]	「チャ」「チュ」「チョ」の子音とほぼ同じ。		church / watch
	[dʒ]	[tʃ]の有声音で、「ヂャ」「ヂュ」「ヂョ」の子音とほぼ同じ。		join / edge
鼻音	[m]	「マ」行子音とほぼ同じ。		meet / time
	[n]	舌の先を上の歯茎につけて、鼻から息を出す。		noon / run
	[ŋ]	[g]を言うつもりで、鼻から声を出す。		thing / song
側音	[l]	必ず舌の先を上の歯茎につける。		late / wall
移行音	[r]	「ウ」のように唇をすぼめる感じで、舌先は歯茎につけない。		red / marry
	[w]	唇をよく丸めて発音する。		way / quick
	[j]	「ヤ、ユ、ヨ」の子音とほぼ同じ。		young / beyond

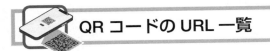

QR コードの URL 一覧

Unit 1	Minako's Role Rob's Role	https://youtu.be/UJ6d6TaKPBQ https://youtu.be/hsergOmG_Fk
Unit 2	Rob's Role Minako's Role	https://youtu.be/ux3UuJWps3M https://youtu.be/WqbpHQc28ww
Unit 3	Rob's Role Justin's Role Minako's Role	https://youtu.be/iCX6XKAqKk0 https://youtu.be/BDNw5zcRhZ4 https://youtu.be/ueP3U3h7jVw
Unit 4	Minako's Role Justin's Role	https://youtu.be/FKqkU1eZ-yA https://youtu.be/WhTl7USSj38
Unit 5	Minako's Role Rob's Role	https://youtu.be/fmY97OEB0xc https://youtu.be/07nV5fwjsJ0
Unit 6	Minako's Role Justin's Role	https://youtu.be/vA9woJc1MZ8 https://youtu.be/hvI2tZ-CdDo
Unit 7	Justin's Role Minako's Role	https://youtu.be/PMBSAPuLI0U https://youtu.be/fW66VB193ko
Unit 8	Minako's Role Justin's Role	https://youtu.be/RMxF6A_fMro https://youtu.be/xzvp-fj-Cws
Unit 9	Justin's Role Professor's Role	https://youtu.be/8zMKa-PjdY4 https://youtu.be/dYmFZ5uWbK8
Unit 10	Minako's Role Justin's Role	https://youtu.be/akYJLQ-u8Cw https://youtu.be/uWZBZEVz5ro
Unit 11	Minako's Role Rob's Role	https://youtu.be/lbH0MTOTEiI https://youtu.be/XgKihefVqFk
Unit 12	Minako's Role Rob's Role	https://youtu.be/GD4enBPdaLg https://youtu.be/uWScMhQjdbs
Unit 13	Justin's Role Minako's Role	https://youtu.be/yncxpe-BV_8 https://youtu.be/_FCz7g1aehA
Unit 14	Rob's Role Minako's Role	https://youtu.be/Q2E03TO_ef8 https://youtu.be/uORlGl_ckaE
Unit 15	Minako's Role Justin's Role	https://youtu.be/JtPJnZrH4nU https://youtu.be/2HO6FAFERqg

TEXT PRODUCTION STAFF

edited by　編集
Minako Hagiwara　萩原 美奈子
Takashi Kudo　工藤 隆志

cover design by　表紙デザイン
Nobuyoshi Fujino　藤野 伸芳

illustration by　イラスト
Yoko Sekine　関根 庸子

CD PRODUCTION STAFF

recorded by　吹き込み者
Jack Merluzzi (AmE)　ジャック・マルージ（アメリカ英語）
Rachel Walzer (AmE)　レイチェル・ワルザー（アメリカ英語）
Yuki Minatsuki (JPN)　水月 優希（日本語）

Let's Read Aloud & Learn English for Science
音読で学ぶ基礎英語《サイエンス編》

2023年1月20日　初版発行
2023年2月15日　第2刷発行

著　者　角山 照彦　Simon Capper

発 行 者　佐野 英一郎

発 行 所　株式会社 成 美 堂
〒101-0052　東京都千代田区神田小川町3-22
TEL 03-3291-2261　FAX 03-3293-5490
https://www.seibido.co.jp

印 刷・製 本　三美印刷株式会社

ISBN 978-4-7919-7263-0　　　　　　　　　　Printed in Japan